Praise for Chef Scottie and Blessed and Highly Flavored Cuisine:

"A Michelin-star like, private dining experience delivered in the comfort of your own home? YES!!!! Chef Scottie, his amazing wife and business partner Lowanda along with his entire Blessed and Highly Flavored Cuisine (BAHFC) team does it ALL with panache! They quietly and skillfully transform your home into a beautiful restaurant complete with amazing place settings and creature comforts that makes you literally want to book reservations to your own house! Before you know it, smooth jazz is gently pumping throughout the place immediately charging the atmosphere – infusing it with expectation – creating the perfect ambiance. When the appetizers start coming from the kitchen, OMG!!! The first thing you notice is the top shelf service, followed by the attention-to-detail, craftsmanship and phenomenal plating. Yes, my friend, it is time to eat! The flavor profiles are eye-popping. And, just when you think you have tasted the best dish of the evening, the Chef serves up another visually pleasing, palate-bursting "foodgasm." Make way Gordon Ramsey, Bobby Flay, Wolfgang Puck and the whole lot of the current famous chefs! Chef

Scottie is the Real Deal – an ascendant culinary master to watch for in the Worldwide Culinary Space. Read his incredible life journey, in his own words, chronicled in this awesome book. Make his dishes from his amazing recipes. However, for maximum enjoyment, book Chef Scottie and his BAHFC team today."

-Todd L. Shuler, Award-winning and Best-Selling Author of the Dew on Ginkgo Leaves series, 10X Rule Coach, Grant Cardone Licensee, Publisher, Serial Entrepreneur, and Investor

"Congrats to Scottie A. Johnson for an amazing event. I highly recommend him for your romantic dinner or your major event. 5 star/excellence!!!" - **Mack McCullough**

"Great job, last night Chef!! You are awesome! Spread Love, the way you and that wonder-filled Wife of yours do! Much Love." - **Chef Curtis Aikens**

"My goodness!!! Your [social media] posts always make me hungry and I'm normally having cereal for dinner. I hope your wife is one of those people that can eat anything and not gain a pound. If not, Lord help her with all that good food." - **Debbie Alexander**

"Your meals look too pretty to eat 😊 😊" - **Denise Gaines**

"Absolutely Fabulous! My wife surprised me with the very special treat of food prepared by Chef Scottie for our anniversary. The Chef and his wife Lowanda made the evening one I'll always rave about. My ribeye was cooked to the perfect temperature, the homemade salad dressing was delicious, the lobster tail stuffed with crabmeat was better than I've been served in four star restaurants, and my taste buds are still longing for more of that off the charts BANANA PUDDING!! The food and intimate service was professionally done from start to finish! We are so looking forward to the next time we get the chance to try more of his dishes!! Thank you, Blessed and Highly Flavored!!!" - **Maurice Randolph**

"Perfection is an understatement!! Amazing cuisine!!!" - **Andrea Felton**

"The Best Chef! And the food? Absolutely amazing!!!" - **Jennifer Hicks**

"Fine dining at its best, in the comfort of your own home!!! Simply amazing!!!" - **April Minger**

"All of the food and service from Chef Johnson was excellent. My family enjoyed every bit of it and can't wait for the next opportunity to use him again. I highly recommend him for your personal chef services."- **Brian Woods**

"Your recipes never cease to amaze me!!!" - **Michelle Webb Parks**

"You have got to experience this wonderful chef's meals. The food was exceptional, from preparation to presentation, very pleasing, I especially enjoyed my stuffed lobster & his own special orange vinaigrette salad dressing. Call this dynamic team and indulge in a great meal you won't regret it! You will be blessed!" - **Beatrice Jackson**

"Looking for a Private Chef??...He is one of the best in Middle Georgia. Private Dinners in the comfort of your home. Birthday Dinner, Anniversary, Just Because... for your boo...Check him out!! Ironically,his roots are from North Carolina and he's a North Carolina Central University Eagle!! Go Scottie A. Johnson, Chef!! - **Donnita Donnette Bellamy**

"Attended a wonderful weekend with this amazing chef. After 20+ years in the military, he started a second career. In such a short time, he has proven himself as a creative, innovative chef. Mr. Johnson did a cooking demonstration as well as providing us with a 4-course meal that was simply amazing, beautiful, and delicious. His presentation was funny and off-the-cuff and quite enjoyable. I highly recommend this personal chef to anyone who wants a first-class meal." - **Debora Ann Johnson**

"I don't know where to begin. Uhmmm, how about the scrumptious mac and cheese??? How about the theme that was fitting for our family? And when I finally tried that gumbo, oooooo Jesus! I was already full while still reaching for my second helping of nana (banana) pudding. Oooooo Jesus!!" - **Joyce Hawkins Woods**

"Would like to Thank Scottie A. Johnson and Lowanda Matthews Johnson for having us over.. The food was AWESOME.. If you are looking for a personal chef, look into Blessed and Highly Flavored Cuisine, it's soooo worth a try. He will not let you down... We had an amazing time... We love you guys!!!!" - **Leslie Hamm**

"THANK YOU Chef Scottie for an amazing evening - best meal we've had in yearsl!! First class operation, and highly recommended." - **David Critten**

"Anyone seeking perfection for a personal dinner or buffet style event Scottie A. Johnson should be your only option!!! Blessed and Highly Flavored Cuisine" - **Grace Cole Woods**

Vision Your Route and Run It:

From Soldier to Award-Winning Chef

Chef Scottie A. Johnson

Contents

Dedication

This book is dedicated to my beautiful wife Lowanda Johnson, who gave me support and inspiration throughout this wonderful journey.

I also dedicate it to my kids, Teri, Brandon, Brittany, Braylon, and my wonderful family. Thank you, Valarie, my sister, and to my aunts and uncles for your help in putting this book together.

A big thank you to my parents, Annie and Ervin Johnson, for instilling in me humbleness and love for God.

Also, I offer this in loving memory of my grandparents, Irvin, Elizabeth, and Lillian, who played a vital part in my life!

Why I Wrote This Book

I've always been a huge fan of great books, and I wanted to do and share things that are near and dear to my heart. Having a passion is just that: a passion. But when you put a vision with that passion, you start to see your love in what you want and/or doing. You see, when your passion and vision start to align then you can run your route. When you pray and ask God for insight on whatever it is you desire and love doing and he shows you a vision (but make sure it's your vision), then you know it's ordained by him. My vision was to be a chef.

Secondly, I wanted to share my story on how it all started, along with some great recipes I love to create as a chef. I feel that behind every recipe is a story to tell about why and how each recipe became important to you. Some of the recipes I've gotten from family — Grandma and them, so to speak! But seriously, most of recipes come from our grandmother, mother, father, or any family member. I like to take them and put my twist on them as chef.

These are a couple of reasons for writing this book, which I will share more deeply in each chapter.

I hope you enjoy the stories and great recipes inside! Blessings upon you!!!

"You have to see the route before you can run it."

About the Chef

Welcome,
My name is Scottie Johnson, and I am a private chef in Warner Robins, Georgia. I was born and raised in Chapel Hill, North Carolina, but became a resident of the great Middle Georgia area by way of the United  States Army. In the Army I served as a 13B cannon crewmember of the Field Artillery branch. I was assigned to the Fort Valley State University's ROTC program as the Senior Military Instructor. After 24 years of great service, I decided to retire and explore my passion of cooking. I enrolled in Helms College Culinary Arts School in Macon, Georgia. It was there where my love for cooking and knowledge of the food industry broadened, and I became more intrigued. I accomplished the art of preparing, cooking, and presenting delectable meals.

Since then I have enjoyed creating various dishes and putting my own unique modifications on traditional dishes. I love cooking with a passion. God has blessed me with this gift of cooking, and I am excited to share this gift with others. I also believe you must have a VISION in life, because without one, you will never move forward!

Upon graduating from Culinary Arts School at the top of my class, I was offered a position as a Chef Instructor Assistant at Helms College. I assisted in teaching multiple classes such as Knife Skills, Cooking Methods and Fabrications, and Restaurant Operations in Helms College's very own Edgar's Bistro. While working at the college, I also started my own private chef business, "Blessed and Highly Flavored Cuisine, LLC". My business offers all the perquisites of elegant fine dining in the comfort of your own home. The thought of making reservations, waiting for seating, and being juggled between tables frustrated me, so I decided to bring all the benefits of fine dining to your home. This way customers can enjoy and experience a delicious, intimate meal created with only them in mind. My cuisine reflects traditional Southern dishes mixed with Cajun flavors and inspired to include gourmet twists. I LOVE what I do!!!

To book Chef Scottie for your next event, please contact him at **sjohn357@gmail.com**. For more details about Blessed and Highly Favored Cuisine, visit **sjcuisine.com**.

Introduction

Ideas and thoughts come and go within our minds! I have learned that whenever I have a thought or idea to quickly write it down or make a note of it immediately. The reason is that if I do not then, every thought, vision, or idea could be lost. Over the years I have experienced quite a few things, and I wanted to share them in this book. I am a chef, and of course I enjoy cooking and creating recipes, or else putting my twist on old family hand-down recipes. Of course, with many recipes comes a story about why each is important or has had a big significance in our life. This book is written to share not only great recipes but also their stories. I never envisioned or thought about becoming a chef as a kid growing up, but I did enjoy food, of course. I became a chef four years ago at the age of 47, enjoying every moment. I decided now at the age of 51 to write this book on my path to where I am today and how I got here! With the support of family, friends, and others, here you go: "Vision Your Route and Run It."

STORY ONE

My Parents' Raising of Me in Love

Growing up in the rural part, or as some would call it, the country part, of Chapel Hill, North Carolina, there was so much to do, but it took your imagination, so to speak. The addresses were route boxes, and most had to walk down long dirt roads or cross the street to get the mail. The homes were a great distance apart from one another, with large back yards to run and play. I remember large fields of cows, chickens, pigs, and anything else you could imagine. The smell would always fill the air and remind you that you were definitely in the country. As a kid, I would visit my cousins down the road or they would come to my house. You see, living in that part of town was family up and down the road. Each house you went to was just like Mom and Dad, so to speak, meaning you were disciplined no matter what.

My sister and I were very fortunate, or blessed, I should say, by having both of our parents raising us and by growing up in a house with both parents together. I know today there are so many broken families, but by the grace of God, they're able to make it. I remember

I would always wonder how it would have been if my parents had divorced during my childhood. You see, family is such a blessing to have and to share all your thoughts, problems, and situations with.

One memory I have is that we would always sit down at the dinner table as a family to eat. We would pray over the great meal that my mom had prepared before eating and talking about our day. During this time, I did not have much to talk about as a kid growing up, but looking back on it, I realized the lesson that was being taught. My father would not say much, but when he did speak, it was powerful and meaningful. My mother would be the one asking questions and bringing up different discussions. I think my sister and I was just like, let us finish eating so we could be excused from the table — of course, this was after we had eaten the food that was on our plate.

The lesson I learned from all the dinnertime discussions was to never be afraid to express what's on your mind. Always know that you can depend on one another in a family. The most important lesson was about communication, which sometimes can be hard to do. There are so many conversations I missed growing up that I think about now because I didn't know how to ask what I needed to know, or I was uncomfortable talking about a subject. My family's dinnertime conversations taught me how to communicate with my own kids now. The dinner table is one of those moments that you can have the entire family together and talk about whatever it is that is on your heart and mind.

My mom was a fantastic cook, and everything she made for dinner was so good! I mean, everything was wonderful, from breakfast to dinner — her eggs, sausage, bacon, homemade biscuits, or salmon patties, all with that good molasses. My father was the pancake guy, and today that's my favorite breakfast! A favorite among my mother's dinners was fried chicken, Southern green beans, sweet potatoes, mac 'n' cheese, and her fantastic potato salad.

Another thing I reflect on that was different for a kid growing up in the country was never going trick-or-treating. My sister and I grew up in the church, and trick-or-treating was not looked at as a favorite or safe thing to do, especially living in the country where no streetlights were in place when it got dark. Costumes played a big part in trick-or-treating as well. Growing up back then as kid in the '80s, costumes required use of your imagination, i.e. Grandma or Mom making a costume out of spare clothing. Now here in the 20th century you can find all sorts of costumes (superheroes, movie characters, sports themes, etc.). Fun times!

I remember when my father cemented me a basketball goal in the back yard so that my friends and I would have something to do. Sports were big thing, and we especially enjoyed imitating famous players. Everyone would come over and we would shoot ball all day long until we got tired. We would play this game called "HORSE." This was a basketball shooting game where each person took turns shooting from different locations at the hoop. If someone made the shot but everyone else missed, they would get a letter in the word "HORSE." The last person left standing wins! One part of the game we would add was dunking the ball, or at least trying! That was all in fun until one day my friend broke the rim dunking and hanging on it. Those were great times.

Sports were fun and very competitive. I remember all the long, hot summers each year playing baseball growing up. I along with my cousins would practice and play numerous games down the street at a park called White Cross. All the players family would be there cheering us on for the big win. Although all of us as teammates were of different races, we were still like a family when at the park playing a game. There was laughter, shouting, crying, and cheering, but never a fight. It was just fun! I was pretty good at baseball as well, along with football and basketball. One great moment was making the all-star team in baseball and traveling to play games. Also as a sophomore (tenth grade, which our high school started at), I made and always played on the varsity team in every sport and lettered each year! Playing sports was a must growing up and we were always competitive.

Church Life

Being raised in the church was a vital part in my life that I always look back on. There were fun times and bad times. The church we grew up in and was baptized in was within walking distance from our house, so we had no excuse for why we could not make it each Sunday. During the summers was one of the highlights of church, VBS, or Vacation Bible School. During these, I remember learning scriptures, eating, and having fun. I also remember getting in trouble at times because I would have too much fun. As kids, we were very involved in church at an early age. We sang in the choir, performed Easter speeches, and ushered. The only thing I would have changed was how long we stayed in church. As a kid, it seemed like service was eight hours long, and then sometimes we had to go back for evening service. I remember sometimes falling asleep in church or not paying attention, and then all of a sudden, there was a hard, quick pinch! Some of you can relate to this happening to you as well.

Easter Sunday was the big church service I can remember. It was not only because of the message but because of the food downstairs in the basement, and especially the new Easter suits, dresses, and baskets for the Easter egg hunt on the Church grounds after service. You could always expect to get a new suit or dress just for that Sunday. As I look back on that, I don't know why that was such a big deal because they would get ruined or dirty running around looking for the eggs. The new shoes would get messed up, too.

Now let us get to the best part, the food downstairs. As a kid, I thought that was some good food we would eat after church. The women would have a spread of food prepared, including fried chicken, baked chicken, roast beef, dumplings, ham, Southern green beans, collard greens, pinto beans, black-eyed peas, butter beans, potato salad, candied yams, cornbread, homemade biscuits, chocolate cake, red velvet cake, sour cream pound cake, pecan pie, sweet potato pie, egg custard pie, chess pie, chocolate pie, peach cobbler, apple cobbler, and so much more! Overall, I have so many great memories of church at an early age. It definitely played a vital part of my life.

My lovely wife, Lowanda and I enjoying dinner

Grandparents' House

Visiting my grandparents' house was a highlight of the day! Most of all my friends growing up could relate to spending time at Grandma and Grandpa's house. As a matter of fact, they pretty much raised us as kids. We lived there until I was four years old along with our parents, but they played an important part in that raising. My parents worked hard every day, and so while they were away, Grandma was there to take care of our every need. The love that I had growing up and being surrounded by a loving family were so important to making me the man I am today. My sister, cousins, and I loved the time we spent there. It was like a going-out-of-town-and-staying-in-a-nice-hotel kind of experience.

The times I spent at my grandparents' house were so much fun! I remember my sister and I would visit and stay with our grandparents everyday in the summertime. One of the things that we would do was spend time in the garden. My granddaddy, as we would call him, would take us out to the garden and show us how to pick vegetables that he was growing. We did not always enjoy going out in the heat, especially as kids working in the garden, but looking back there were many lessons we learned from my grandfather. As we picked the green beans, tomatoes, snap peas, and so much more, I would be wondering when we would finish so we could go back inside to the AC.

Little did I know that upon our return inside the house there was something great waiting for us. My grandma would always have a pleasant lunch waiting for us to eat. This time would allow us to sit down as family and have some fantastic conversations. Often these would of course be about the garden. I remember one thing we would do during that time with my granddaddy was watch the soap operas while we ate lunch. We would watch The Young and the Restless every day with him, and I have been hooked since then. I find myself remembering those times as I continue to watch at this present day. The little things that we seemed to forget are so much the bigger things that we need this present day. It molded us into who and what we are today.

Another great memory was my grandfather's infamous fish fry. I remember the one time I went fishing off the pier with my grandfather and my Aunt Billie on the coast of Carolina. It was a very cold early morning as we left to go fishing off the pier. I remember being loaded down with cold weather gear to the point I could hardly move, but I was so excited to be going fishing. I do not recall catching anything, but the memory was what stuck with me. It felt important, being a part of something that was a tradition in preparing for all the wonderful fish fries. The conversation I had with my grandfather and aunt was very important, and as a kid, I found myself listening with both ears.

Every summer or fall, my grandfather would get the pot out and cleaned in preparation for the big fish fry. This was a family-effort type of event so everyone pitched in to help. My father, grandfather, uncles, and others would clean all the fish, season them, and get them ready to fry. Spot, a small saltwater type of fish, made up the bulk of what was caught and fried. My grandmother was inside with the other women preparing all the side items, like potato salad, baked beans, salad, coleslaw, and stuff. Oh, yeah, I cannot forget about the homemade hush puppies and all the great desserts, which were my favorite part, of course! The South was big on desserts, and so was my family. I mean, just the smell of fish and hush puppies being fried, desserts baking in the oven, sun tea brewing, and lemonade sweating in the sun, along with the fun of seeing family and friends of the neighborhood all enjoying great food, fellowship, laughter, and conversations, made everything spectacular.

Not only did the fish fry bring lots of fun to my grandparents' house, but so did the huge family reunions. Our family was so big that my sister and I did not know each cousin, aunt, uncle, or friend, but we still had a great time. You see, food was and will always be a significant part of our life. With every dish, there is "Food for Thought." I will talk more about that later in the chapters. Family reunions were a time that everyone got together and reminiscenced about old times, listened to great music, and enjoyed awesome food, and as a kid, I loved listening to the older generation tell their inflated stories. We did not know that for a long time until my mom would say, "Stop believing that mess you hear." The words "This is old folk conversation" would be the sign to leave and go play. There were a couple more memories at my grandparents' house to share with you.

The holidays were the best of times at my grandparents' house. The one of many things I remember was Christmas. Man, that was a time as kids we would look forward to every year. You see, getting gifts was something that we could not wait for, and we loved the enjoyment of opening them. I recall my sister and I would get the Sears catalog and circle all the toys we wanted. As a matter of fact, we would fight over who had the book to circle our stuff first. The Christmas catalog was one of the highlights during the holidays for my sister and me. It was something about opening up the catalog and flipping through the pages to see all the toys, electronics, and anything else that excited us. I recall one Christmas we were sitting in the living room with the fire going in the fireplace as we opened up our gifts that was under the tree. My dad yelled out to me to go check the door because there was somebody knocking, and of course I did not want to leave what I was doing — plus, I didn't hear anybody knocking. I went to the door anyway to open and didn't see anyone, but out of excitement my eyes got big because of what I did see. As I looked with shock and excitement, I saw a go-kart. Wow, a small racing car to a kid was the best! That was a great moment!

That go-kart was the best Christmas gift ever. Despite the cold weather, I put on my coat and went outside to ride it. That was a fun time, and of course, my sister wanted to join in on the fun, and I did not want her to, but I did. You see, my sister and I are only a year and month apart. She was born February 1969 and I was born March 1968. So I decided to let her ride one day in the back yard and told her to be careful and made sure she knew how to drive it. I will never forget that moment when she rode it and could not stop, which ended up terribly. She ran into the clothesline pole and bent the front of my go-kart. I was so mad!!! She started crying, but I was not concerned with that — only my go-kart being messed up. This again was another great memory. I think I was around 13 years old. Man, those were the good old days. My sister and I shared a lot of great times together being that she was my only sister.

Going back to my grandparents' house, I recall some other great memories with my cousins. We were so close you would think we were all sisters and brothers. I was the only male growing up, and so I got a lot of special treatment, and my sister and cousins could not stand it. Christmas at grandma's house was special. All the adults would go out shopping then come home to wrap the presents to put under the tree. The stack of gifts was exciting to see. The one thing we would love to do is try to guess what was gift-wrapped up. We would make a game out of it, as we would anything else. We would go so far as to look or snoop around the rooms in the house and find stuff that had not been wrapped yet. If we found we would tell one another, "I know what you are getting for Christmas." We would sneak under the tree and open up the gift then re-wrap it. Of course, everyone would know what we did, but it was so much fun. Like I said, being at my grandparents' house brought lots of joy and laughter among all of us kids.

Hillsborough, North Carolina, which was where my grandparents lived, was a place where you experienced love and warmth from everyone within the community. My grandmother and grandfather were two people who were well known in town. My grandmother was a seamstress, and she did it with passion and love. My grandfather worked at the mill in town. I remember one day my sister, he, and I walked all the way from the house in town to the mill where he worked. We were young, and I recall it being a long walk, but seeing him do it gave me the mindset that I could do it, too. I guess it was just the quality time we spent with our grandparents that made waking up each day a pleasant one and something to look forward to. You see, being apart from my family and missing out on so much quality time with many were sacrifices that played a major part in my life, which is something I will get into later in this book. The military life! Family is so very important as a kid growing up. We all as kids come up from different parts of this world.

I was blessed to have both my grandmothers when I was coming up as kid unto adulthood. The funny thing about that is my sister and I would refer to them as Grandma Hillsborough (my dad's mom) and Grandma Chapel Hill (my mom's mother). The one thing they both had in common was cooking great suppers, which is what they called it back then. We — well, I — refer to them as dinner now. But they knew how to throw down in the kitchen. You see, back then they cooked with nothing but the freshest ingredients, and most of it came from the gardens. The hours they put in the kitchen were unbelievable. We would always wonder how they had an entire Sunday dinner prepared when we came back home from church. I now realize it was because they got up early in the morning and prepared it — not to mention breakfast as well. Some of us come up with lots of money and some with little or none at all. But there is one thing I do see in common with many people, and that is the fact that we spent so much of our life at grandparents' house, and that is where we learned the meaning of the love of a family! My grandparents have now passed, but they left so many memories to reflect back on, and its what I call now a legacy!

High School

As I move forward to my high school days, there were a lot of great times and memories I can reflect back on. We were raised and lived in the country of Chapel Hill, North Carolina. A car or bus was transportation back and forth to school, or we would catch a ride with a cousin down the street. This was back in the '80s, and I graduated high school in 1986. High school then was grades ten through twelve. Now currently high school starts in the ninth grade for most. I was crazy about sports, so of course that was the highlight of high school. My friends and I started school with the mindset that we wanted to try out for the varsity team, not junior varsity. I made the varsity in every sport that I played, and these included football, basketball, and track and field. Not only did I make the varsity, but also I was a starter, so that was extremely exciting. We had only one high school and it was called Chapel Hill High "Tigers." I will come back to sports, but the thing I remember most was the friends I made.

Being in the tenth grade, my high school was a little intimidating because remember I mentioned that was the beginning of high school in the '80s. I saw the seniors walking around proudly seeing it was their last year. Sometimes we would have to prove ourselves to walk the same hallways they did or to eat in the cafeteria, but sports was my way of fitting in. I did not take my tenth-grade year seriously when it came to my classes and homework until I had to attend summer school that year. That was a huge revelation, especially if I wanted to continue to play sports. So my following year up until I graduated, I buckled down. I'm not saying it was easy, and I definitely was not on the "A" honor roll, but I did graduate on time with my Class of 1986. High school and college were two of the most important parts of growing up into adulthood.

The sports life was huge in my high school growing up. As I mentioned earlier, it was a highlight of each day. I recall the day I tried out for the football varsity team my first year in high school. It was very intimidating knowing that I was competing against others who were one to two years ahead of me. Also, since we had only one high school, that made it much more competitive to make the team.

Along with my friends and a few cousins, we went to the tryouts and made the varsity team. I was excited and knew that was a huge accomplishment for me and all my family to see. Football was huge in North Carolina! I knew it was not going to be easy, but I just wanted to do the best I could and of course have fun. I played wide receiver and defensive back, rotating back and forth as a starter. You see, back then it was not unusual for a player to play both offense and defense. It was more than playing football, basketball, or running track. It was about the camaraderie and the discipline we got from the coaches. They were like a mom or dad while on the field or court. Hard work was unavoidable because you had to put in what you wanted to get out from it. I remember all the long practices every day after school. I remember the the two three-a-day practices during the hot summer days. We poured our sweat and tears on the field as we perfected our skills.

Friday mornings came, and that was an exciting and important day of the week: game day! I remember getting up and getting dressed in a suit and tie because that was one of the things we did together as a team. It also let all the students see that we were representing them and the school, whether it was a home or away game. It made me feel important walking the hallways, sitting in the classroom dressed up in a suit and tie or our letterman jackets. It also reminded me of all the hard work I put in during the days leading up to Friday. You see there should always be a reminder of what you are trying to accomplish because it's your VISION of where you're going or want to go! I would hear friends saying, "Good luck," "Have a great game," "We are cheering you on," and so much more. It made you feel special and loved because to be honest not everyone was able to do it. For whatever reason, it was special — a day to look forward to: game night. This was something all of us looked forward to, even the families and teaching staff. Everything was set to play, and the fun was about to happen! Friday game night was here, and the excitement just went up ten notches! As I remember all the practices, as well as the mental, physical, and emotional things I went through up to this point, I knew that I was prepared for Friday night football! And then, pon graduating from high school, there was another adventure to conquer. College!

STORY TWO

The Departure

College Life

Starting college was exciting and nerve-wracking. My sister and I were very fortunate and blessed to have parents who worked like crazy for us to be able to attend college. Of course, I graduated high school a year before my sister did, so I was the first in the boat attending college, and all eyes of my family were on me. Upon starting college, I had some anxieties because of all the unknowns. Who were the people I would call my friends? What group or groups would I associate with or just hang out with? The one thing I did know was that I could not mess this opportunity up with the wrong decisions.

But let's back up a moment to when I was looking at colleges to attend. Of course there were certain schools that were interested in me to play football and receive some type of scholarship. I remember my dad and I would take trips to visit various colleges and check out the football programs. I was not thinking about the educational part of it, just playing football. Some of the colleges where I was invited were James Madison

University, Livingstone College, Catawba College, Liberty College and a few more. Some of my high school teammates had already chosen their colleges, and some got full scholarships, but for me it was different.

When I say it was different, I am talking about the reason I chose a different college. I was not looking at it to play football, but for a very different reason: my girlfriend! Do not get me wrong; college football was still a desire of mine to play, but like all young men, I had other things on my mind. Therefore, I decided to attend North Carolina Central University in Durham, North Carolina. This college was about 25-30 minutes from my house and my girlfriend at the time. Therefore, I enrolled in NCCU, "The Eagles," and started my freshman year.

I enjoyed my freshman year, but there was so much to learn and at a very fast pace. Being a freshman in college was like starting all over again, just as it was in high school. The difference in college from high school was that you were on your own. There was no teacher in the hallway telling you to get in your classroom or asking if you needed something. This was something new that I had to get used to. My freshman year I stayed on campus in the dormitory called Chidley Hall. This was the only male dorm on the campus, and it was all alone on top of what we called the hill. You see, all the buildings that housed my classes were down the hill in what we referred to as "the bowl." We called it that because as you looked down from the dorm it resembled a bowl.

This was something that I had to get use to doing, getting up and walking down to my classes. It became easier as time went by, and I was doing it very well. Nevertheless, as time went by I would find myself checking out different campus parties where there were a lot of females and alcohol. Some people would say that is the "college life," but my parents and grades said different. In between trying to see my girlfriend, classes, parties, and all the running around, I saw me falling in my class work. In addition, I was looking to play football, which was still a desire of mine to do. Therefore, I decided to pursue that desire!

I went to visit the football staff and introduce myself to everyone and state my desire to play. So I was introduced to all the players and was paired with a couple of wide receivers to train with during camp. It was very different on the college level than high school, but football is football. I loved being back in the weight room and in the field running routes, along with all the training and workouts. One of the receivers I had a pleasure of training with was Robert Clark, who is a former professional American football wide receiver in the National Football League back in 1987-95. Football was sport I fell in love with.

One reason was that my cousin, Denise was married to an American football player, Louis Breeden, who played defensive back for the Cincinnati Bengals in the National Football League. He was someone I admired and would take some football skill notes from. And being part of the family had its rewards as well! Our family was huge on sports and supported me playing. My mom, on the other hand, was a typical mom, always worried about me getting hurt on the field. However, needless to say, despite the colleges everyone had attended, we all were on one accord when it came to a team: the University of North Carolina Tarheels. We are and will always be die-hard Tarheel fans!

Going back to my college days at North Carolina Central University was the start of an amazing journey. I think the hardest parts of college were the courses and class schedules. I remember having a few classes in the evenings and sometimes at night. I would sometimes skip out on those. I mean, having a 7 p.m. or 8 p.m. biology lab class was just right wrong! I struggled making that particular class, which indeed affected my overall GPA and my playing football. There were so many distractions in college with parties, females, sports, and so much more that made it sometimes difficult to focus.

Because my grades started to fall, football, fraternities, and other stuff had to be put on hold, which took me to the start of another journey.

I decided to join the military, and specifically the Army Reserves. One of my friends in college and I had registered for an ROTC class next door at Duke University. At first, we liked going to class and learning all the things about the military, but as it went on we decided to pursue it in a different way, joining the Army Reserves. Therefore, we enlisted and went through all the requirements that needed to be done. I was excited and again at the same time nervous of the unknown. Of course, I would talk with my father about it since he was a veteran Army paratrooper. So again, I was venturing out to something exciting and away from friends. Now came the huge test, basic training, in the year 1987.

Shipping off to basic training was the scariest thing I had ever done in my young life at the time. Now all the fun began! As I am writing this, I remember vividly of everything that took place in basic training. Let me share with you my experience of basic training back in 1987 at Fort Sill, Oklahoma. First, leaving my family, friends and girlfriend at the time was hard, and especially leaving my parents and sister. My sister and I are very close, not to mention again that we are only a year and a month apart. But I was raised in a strong, spiritual, God-fearing household, so I that made the transition a little more easily.

I remember the airplane ride and then the long bus ride to basic training. That was the relaxing part, until we got off the bus, and then reality hit quick and hard. The first time I laid eyes on the drill sergeant or drill instructors back then were a memory that would be embedded in my mind forever. We got off the bus and immediately were met by the drill sergeants. We ended up face down on rocks and gravel doing push-ups until our hands had imprints of each and every rock on the ground, not to mention we had duffel bags on our backs, which added more weight. I wanted to cry and started thinking, "What did I get myself into?" Nevertheless, what made me more and more calm was the fact that everybody was going through the same thing.

As time went on, basic training became tolerable and quite a few times exciting. Each day was the same waking up, doing strenuous exercises, showering, and eating breakfast, and then it was on to training, followed by lunch, dinner and lights out. The next day was the same, so we adjusted quickly to everything. My MOS, which stands for Military Occupational Specialty, was Field Artillery Cannon Crewmember (13B). We stayed in the field learning various skill-level specialties. I started to have fun as time went along, and we became a family away from family. I started to notice as time went by and we moved to other phases, the drill sergeants would ease up just a little, which was quite fine to us!

I was gone for about 14-15 weeks before graduating and returning back home to North Carolina. Graduation was a special and exciting day. It was a day of being proud of all my accomplishments and the fears I had overcome. It was the day that I became soldier in the United States Army Reserves. Now here it is again that I was sad about leaving another family I had become close to in basic training/AIT. You see, we all went through the same things throughout basic training, and whether good or bad, easy or hard, they made us stronger. We built relationships that were stronger than anything else. It was an instance that gave me a different outlook on things. It matured me and taught me responsibility. My father instilled many things in my early childhood and this just capitalized it!

Upon graduating Basic Training/AIT, I returned home back to my family. That was a great day to see my parents, my sister, and of course my girlfriend. I remember upon returning home I was surprised with my first car. It was a brand new white Nissan 200SX. Although my sister and I would have to share it, taking turns who would drive, I was determined that I would use the older brother thing and have it more. We were very fortunate and blessed! Everyone was so glad to see me return home from basic training, and I was just as excited to see everyone as well. I knew that there would be lots of questions that my family and friends would have, so I just prepared myself for them and of course gave them what they wanted. Another great moment and memory to look back on.

Now returning to college, I had a different mindset and outlook. I came back with a brand new attitude on life. The things I had experienced, physically, mentally, spiritually, and emotionally, were much bigger and greater than football in college. I had a positive attitude about everything and would let nothing get me down. The military did something to me, and I did not realize it until I returned to college. Now this was the first of many experiences that proved the military had done something to me, which I will explain later. Going into my next semester of college, I left the dorm life, returned home, and just commuted back and forth because I had a brand new car to drive. I continued at North Carolina Central University for a year and half before realizing that I wanted to switch my major to one they did not offer

I was majoring in criminal justice at North Carolina

Central University at the time, but I became interested in mechanical engineering. I think it may have been because of Uncle Sanders, my dad's brother who attended North Carolina Agricultural and Technical State University, which, by the way, was our rival. My uncle obtained his mechanical engineering degree from there and was working as a mechanical engineer. I decided that was what I wanted to now study, but I didn't want to attend a four-year college, so I transferred in 1989 to a two-year college, Alamance Community College. This college was about twenty-five minutes from home, which made it easy to get back and forth. They did not offer engineering so I studied and received my Associate of Applied Science degree (A.A.S) in mechanical drafting and design. I really enjoyed going to a community college, and most of my credits transferred, so that was great.

Community College was less stressful and got to the meat and potatoes of my major. It was more technical, and I am a hands-on learning person, and that is what I got from Alamance Community College. They did not have a football team at the time, but that was not necessary to me. I was enjoying going to class and learning all about drafting. The math part of it was sometimes challenging, but I found myself enjoying it and doing well in the classes. There were limited distractions during my time in community college, and I took every advantage of it. My class schedule was perfect and allowed me time to commute back and forth from home. That was a plus in itself.

As I continued going to school, I secretly got married. For the longest time, both our parents did not know because I was still living at my parents' house. It was crazy! I finally graduated and all my family was there for the graduation, and so was my wife whom no one knew. I guess it was kind of an adventurous thing we did and keeping it a secret until the right time made it more and more exciting. Now here again I was about to start another journey in my life. Nevertheless, before graduating I had to do an internship. I was selected to work with the City of Graham, North Carolina, in its civil engineering department. I was interning with a team doing survey work. You see them in the yellow vehicle on the sides of the road and measuring, sighting distances for the construction of building roads. It was a unique job because we were outside most of the time and got to see different people.

I did such a great job that upon graduating I was offered a permanent position working for the State of North Carolina in civil engineering as a surveyor. It was a great job. Now, as time went along, the secret was out about our marriage, and eventually I was out of my parents' house and living with my wife at the time. As time went along, we had a daughter, Teri Alexis Johnson. My wife at the time also had a daughter, Danielle, by her previous marriage, and I accepted her as my own. Teri got her first name from her grandfather, whose last name was Terry. Her middle name, Alexis, was the same as mine. I always wondered how names come about, especially mine. I just wanted to share that! I continued to work, attend to my Army Reserve obligations, and enjoy being a family.

It was 1994 that I wanted something more and better to support my family. Do not get me wrong; I enjoyed my job but just wanted something different, long term. My wife oldest brother was in the Army at the time, and I started talking with him about going from the Army Reserves to active duty. I was mostly looking at all the benefits and being able to travel. The good thing was switching from the reserves to active was easy and convenient. I would not have to do anything as far as basic training. I would keep my current military occupational specialty, or MOS, and the best part of it was that I did not have to start over again. Since I had a college degree, I could go in active as a specialist (E4) rather than private. That was the clincher, and I made the decision to go active duty.

STORY THREE

Lifetime Military Experiences

So then, it was still 1994, and I went from the Army Reserves to active duty. I made this decision because I wanted more for my family and all the benefits that came with it. I was blessed to be stationed just under a two-hour drive to Fort Bragg, North Carolina. I was excited about leaving and starting another journey in the military but not so excited that my family could not go with me right away because of school and work, and I needed to find housing. Eventually they would join me in Fort Bragg, which was my first duty station and close to home. There were some challenges, some difficulties, some heartache, and some good times.

You see, the military at some times can be a load or put a strain on families, but it was something that we would have to get use to and try to overcome. Being active duty now was exciting, knowing that I could better support my family who were at the time back in Burlington, North Carolina. I lived the barracks life at the beginning until I found an apartment or house for us all to live in. It was hard being away from my family in the beginning until I made a routine for myself each day, plus keeping myself busy. This was the beginning of what the military dealt to me: sacrifice! I would of course every weekend drive home to see my family if there wasn't any field training going on or I wasn't on any type of duty cycles. You see, being a 13B field artillery soldier, we spent a lot of time in the field on training exercises. I had flashbacks of basic training because again I made more friends and a family away from my real family. I had to get used to getting up every morning. My day would start off with waking up bright and early in the morning and doing physical training — PT is what it was called. After that was conducting personal hygiene and going to the mess hall for some good military breakfast. Then came formations that started whatever was on the training calendar for the day.

Each day was the same, and every week repeated itself, so it became a routine for me. The one thing you knew that would take place was our morning PT and motor pool Mondays. Every Monday was an entire day in the motor pool, which is where we would conduct all the preventive maintenance checks and services. PMCS is what we called it. All of our equipment, including vehicles, radios, field gear, howitzers, and personal gear would be checked for proper maintenance and kept in working order. You see, everything needed to be always ready for training and real war deployments. The motor pool was a full day each Monday with our first formation of the day and our last formation of the day before being released to enjoy the rest of the day, evening, and night.

And now the sacrifices would start! Before my family and I were reunited, it wasn't a problem going to the field for weeks at a time, working long days, and having some type of duty, because I was by myself. But now the family had come, and sacrifices began. I would now have to prepare myself and my family each time I was in the field training or on an exercise somewhere. It was hard being away from them, but this was the start of many more challenges to come. The life of being in the Army was now the beginning of starting a military career and a very exciting one as well. Fort Bragg, North Carolina, was my first duty station from 1994 to 1997. I would then move on to the next one.

Now it was 1997 and I was off to my next duty station, Fort Hood, Texas. Again I would undergo PCS, or permanent change of station, which is the assignment, detail, or transfer of a member or unit to a different duty station under orders, not knowing what to expect. Being stationed at one place for a long period of time, you get used to how it operated and used to the other soldiers. It was always one thing each of us would experience being at a new duty station — nervousness. I was also worried about the fact that I would be under a new command and unit. Now I would have to build and gain camaraderie with new people. The excitement was always something to look forward to when it was time to PCS.

Fort Hood is a military post located in Killeen, Texas, and it is a huge installation as well. Fort Hood is the only post in the United States capable of stationing and training two armored divisions. It was huge! I remember the day I left North Carolina traveling to Texas. I remember it because my father took the trip with me. We drove eighteen hours, just the two of us. That was a father-and-son time we spent that stuck with me all of my life. I had heard a lot about Fort Hood and was looking forward to being stationed there. The trip there with my father was great, despite the eighteen hours. We enjoyed the drive along with some great conversations and frequent stops for food and gas.

Once we arrived at Fort Hood, it was a day before my actual reporting day. We checked into a hotel, got settled in, and then proceeded on base to check things out and see the exact location I needed to report to the next day. Basically, I was using what the Army had taught me, how to recon. Once we got familiarized with everything, we left base to get something to eat and then settle in for the night. I enjoyed that time I had with my father, as I still do. We found a restaurant to have dinner and then went back to the room to rest for the night while watching a television or probably more of the television watching us. It was a very long day of traveling. We awoke the next morning and my father was off to the airport to go back home, and I reported to my unit. It was the beginning of my Fort Hood experience and my second duty station.

I was now at the in-processing center to find out which unit I was going to be working. By surprise I was called to the replacement first sergeant's office for some reason. After meeting with the first sergeant, I was informed that I would be working under right there in replacement. You see, my 13B MOS was over strength at the time, meaning there wasn't a slot for me, so I filled a position there, in-processing non-commissioned officers and commissioned officers. When I say that was a blessing, is an understatement. Leaving Fort Bragg, North Carolina, where I was constantly in the field training, would result in a break at Fort Hood replacement.

Of course this new job was great, but it had a few obstacles, which is in any job you do. I was a sergeant, in-processing people who out-ranked me on a daily basis. There were lots of days I would be intimated because I had to brief and give classes to senior enlisted and above. The replacement center was your first stop before going to your unit. It was here where you got briefed on policies, medical procedures, transportation, and so on. It was also where you received your unit assignment, which quite often the person didn't agree with. Eventually it started to become easy and comfortable for me to conduct my briefings and classes. I also had some great supervisors and staff looking out for me and helping me.

Being stationed at Fort Hood was fun and exciting. The fact it was Central Texas made it a plus as well. It was in close proximity to all major cities across the state. The nearest was Austin, but Dallas, Houston, San Antonio and San Marcos weren't far at all and within driving distance from Killeen, which is the city where Fort Hood is located. Work wasn't at all stressful or hard, but it was surprisingly great to wake up and go to for a change. It had its days, but the majority of time it was great. My wife and at the time my brother were stationed in San Antonio, so I would sometimes drive to spend weekend there. My family did not come with me to Fort Hood, and due to other issues, we eventually got divorced. Life happens, but through it all God was always watching over me and keeping me safe.

Again I considered and saw myself as being blessed. I was a field artillery soldier working at a replacement center where no field exercises (FTX) were conducted, so my evenings and weekends were mine to do what I wanted. I met some great people and made lots of friends. I became really close to my team at work, and we would hang out lots of the time, eventually becoming a family. Since they were higher ranking than me, they would always be looking out for me and guiding me in the right directions, while keeping me on the path. Sometimes it's hard to find people in your corner who have your best interests at heart and are not trying to keep you down and keep you from advancing in promotions. I was blessed to have supportive friends.

There were times I would miss my 13B job and going to the field. There were times I would even miss the weeklong training. For members of the field artillery branch, there was a bond that couldn't be broken. It was similar to the bond members of the infantry had with each other. But then came an opportunity that I couldn't resist. There were some slots that needed NCOs to in-process personnel coming into Bosnia. That was my job I was doing in replacement, so I volunteered. Of course I would get comments from my friends about going, but it was something I wanted to do, and it would also be great in military records for promotion. I was now looking to advance up in rank because I had another journey I wanted to fulfill.

I got selected to deploy to Bosnia and began all the necessary training that needed to be done. It was 1998, and I was about to conduct my first deployment, not knowing I would have plenty more to come. The training went well, and everything that needed to be done was completed successfully. The day came for me to deploy, and I was excited and afraid at the same time. Again, not knowing what to expect was the scary part, but doing something none of my friends from home were doing made it exciting. Also, I was motivated by the fact that my father, who had served in the Army, would be proud of me as well. The fact that I was single made it easy to leave, but I would still miss my family. It was only a planned six-month deployment, which ended up longer, but I experienced so many things while deployed that matured me in so many ways and prepared me for what was to come further in my career.

Like I mentioned earlier, this was my first of many deployments, so upon returning I would have a lot of questions asked. I returned back to my unit and fell right back in place. I eventually got married again and had kids — twins, as a matter of fact, a boy and a girl. I was a family again with more responsibility, but I continued to enjoy life. Now I had three kids, two daughters and one son. I will talk more about my kids later in the book, but for now, on to my next journey. One of my platoon sergeants use to be a drill sergeant, and as I would look at the drill sergeant badge she wore on her uniform it stood out to me. It inspired me, and so I started looking into becoming a drill sergeant and asking questions. The more and more I researched, I knew that was something I wanted to do.

Now the only thing that was holding me back was my rank. You see, I was a sergeant, SGT/E5, and one of the requirements needed at the time was a rank of staff sergeant, SSG/E6. Of course it was a little disappointing, but I knew what I had to do before submitting my packet. I needed to get promoted, so I started studying for the promotion board. I would continue to take classes and correspondence courses to give me points and everything else needed. My work team again came to the rescue by making sure I was prepared for the promotion board. I eventually went to board and passed, now making me a SGT(P)/ promotable. I can't remember what the points were for promotion at that time, but eventually I had enough points to be promoted to SSG/E6.

Now I was ready to embark on another career move,

drill sergeant school. I resubmitted my packet for school and waited patiently for a response. As time went by, I received an email referencing my packet, and I was informed I had been selected for the drill sergeant school. I was excited about the news and surely looked forward to attending. After receiving the news, I started preparing myself by asking former drill sergeants that I worked with how the school was. There was something about wearing that badge of a drill sergeant on my uniform and also helping with promotion. It was the thought of being able to train other young men and women in becoming a soldier. Now was the time to challenge myself, and I knew it wasn't going to be easy attending drill sergeant school, but I was ready!

Again it was time for another permanent change of station (PCS). I left Fort Hood, Texas, en route to Fort Leonard Wood, Missouri, to attend drill sergeant school. It was a long eleven-hour drive there, but it was well worth it. As I packed up my car and got on the road to Missouri, I reflected on all the things I had done thus far in my military career and the fact that I was now about to embark on another one. Not knowing what to expect at school, there was a moment of excitement and nervousness, but with challenges they both come together. I finally made it to Fort Leonard Wood and signed in to the reception station. As I looked around at all the others who were there for the same thing, drill sergeant school, I saw the same look in their faces as mine. We received our brief and were assigned our rooms. That night I intentionally made an effort to make friends and get acquainted.

After staying up and talking with everyone, it was time to settle in my room and get some rest for the early morning. As I lay in bed, my mind started to wonder about what was going to take place the next morning. The not knowing was something that I had gotten quite used to, so I closed my eyes and got the much-needed rest. The morning came, and I did all the necessary things and reported downstairs. As I looked around at all the other groups of us, we all had that look on our face — what did we get ourselves into? Wow, it was like being back in basic training all over again. I had flash-backs on everything as soon as the drill instructors came and took over. The in-processing went smoothly but seemed too quiet, so I knew that it was the calm before the storm.

After we finished in-processing and getting all our briefs, it was game on. We were divided into platoons and squads and assigned our drill instructors. Each day was just like being back in basic training but on anoth-er level. We had to learn everything but in a way to be able to teach others in a basic training unit. All of that wasn't bad, but the most stressful part being in drill sergeant school was learning and reciting the modules! I had a book of modules that I was supposed to learn and pitch back to the instructors. The good thing was that we were paired up with a battle buddy, and that's who we spent the majority of our time with in the evenings after class. We would get together and study our modules for the next day. Passing the modules was a requirement to graduate. But there was a surprise to pitching each module.

When the time came to pitch our modules, we had to draw a card not knowing which module we had to pitch, so it was important to study each of them. The key thing that our drill instructor told us was that it was vital that both of us knew the module. The reason for that was because when one is pitching it, the other must do it by the numbers or whatever instructional method was used. If one of us said something that wasn't right then the other would make a movement or not, which would jog the memory. Some students would take their chances and play Russian roulette, so to speak, and not study the hard modules thinking they wouldn't pick it. In this school you couldn't rely on that, because it never failed that you would draw the module you didn't study.

Once I got the routine down it would become easy, training my mind to retain the information. One way of doing that was talking to trees. It wasn't a shock to see someone talking to a tree because in school that's what was needed to get through it. I would quite often talk to myself while walking, running, at the tree, even on the toilet. We weren't going crazy but just training our minds to retain each line of the modules and learn what method of instruction to pitch it. You see, everything we learned in the military was taught to us by some kind of instruction — for instance, drill and ceremony. From marching to saluting, there was a method of instruction. Then of course we had to learn the drill sergeant creed! It's amazing how much the human brain can retain, and we definitely found that out in drill sergeant school.

As I went on through the school, I started having fun and making great friends. We had some great drill instructors over our platoon. I also had the opportunity to get certified in lots of things. The one that stood out was master fitness trainer. I had the luxury of being selected to attend master fitness school while in drill sergeant school. Master fitness trainer school was a beast. We had to learn the entire anatomy of the body. We had to run like crazy and learn all the different stretches and exercises on a master fitness level. Of course our physical fitness test needed to be the maximum in each event with a total score of 300. This was the APFT standard back in 1999 when I went to drill sergeant school. I was a physically, mentally, and spiritually fit after school.

It was now time for graduation, and what a day of excitement it was. The moment came that we were given our drill sergeant hat and badge. That was a great feeling to wear the hat and, more important, earning it! After graduating I quickly packed my car and got on the road to head back to my duty station. As I drove the long eleven hours back, I just reflected on everything and how proud I was of myself for accomplishing another great journey. Becoming a drill sergeant was something I always wanted to do. It was a job not everyone could do or get selected to do. The military would say only the top 10 percent would be selected, and that's how I felt! It wasn't feeling like I was superior, but I experienced a feeling of boldness! I had accomplishing something that was intimidating!

After graduating from drill sergeant school, I was assigned to Fort Sill, Oklahoma, for my two-year drill sergeant duty. Fort Sill was home of the Artillery back in 1999, and being a 13B, I was right at home. I arrived at Fort Sill and checked in at the in-processing center and then reported to my unit. It felt good and proud to now be a drill sergeant and able to wear my drill sergeant hat. This was the start of a long, busy two-year assignment, but I was excited and looking forward to it. As I learned the ropes and how everything went, I became quite comfortable with my team. We had a great unit and the training was exactly what I expected. I was now on the other side, meaning I wasn't the trainee but the trainer. It was definitely a task in the beginning because my job now was to take a young kid and basically make him/her a soldier.

When I got to Fort Sill in 1999, it was OSUT, One Station Unit Training, meaning we as drill sergeants would teach the trainees basic and advanced individual training for the 13B cannon crewmember military occupational specialty. After about a year it became just BCT, basic combat training, as we only trained the basic combat skills needed no matter the MOS. After they completed basic training, they would travel to their assigned MOS duty station. At the beginning we only trained males, but after my first year we received females as well. Having females to train was a task that we as drill sergeants needed to be educated on. All were looked at as soldiers but had differences as well that were important. There were a few issues at the beginning, but they all got worked out, and training was on one accord.

Drill sergeant duty was a two-year assignment, and every second of each day was filled with work. It was a duty assignment that required long hours and sacrifices, especially if you had a family. When I left for work my kids were asleep, and most of the time when I returned home from work they were in bed. There would be times when I would be so tired that I would fall asleep at the dinner table or even sometimes at the stop light for a second or two. I'm talking about sixteen- to eighteen-hour days, seven days a week. We would rotate the weekends with our battle buddies in the platoon. Another thing was having CQ duty, or charge of quarters. For this, a drill sergeant had to guard and take care of the unit for twenty-four hours until relieved the next morning once the first drill came in. We would just watch over the office and barracks throughout the night.

Now imagine coming in around 4:30 in the morning and not getting off until the next morning. You would still have to train the soldiers all day, plus pull your CQ duty — a long day! We got smart after a while and came up with a solution within our platoon. We decided that whoever had CQ would not come in until noon, which helped out tremendously. As a drill sergeant we were responsible for teaching them how to march, as well as physical fitness, basic rifle marksmanship, drill and ceremony, uniform wear — basically everything. Basic training was about nine weeks long, and every week featured different types of training, so it was always move, move, and move. Everything had a sense of urgency, but there was also an urgent need to remain safe. Once the nine-week cycle was over, we would get a new group in and do it all over again.

Sometimes we would have a two-week break in between cycles, but quite often there was less than a week. I would look forward to the cycle breaks because that was time to be with family, and for rest and relaxation. Most of the time we would travel to the next city or somewhere close, just to get away for awhile. Fort Sill was located in Lawton, Oklahoma, so we weren't too far from Wichita Falls, Texas, or Oklahoma City, Oklahoma. Just to get away for a minute was great, and to spend time with family was most important. The cycle breaks would go by so quickly, and before you knew it, it was time to go back to work. We would have to come in a few days early before picking up the new group in order to get our platoon bays ready. We would paint, clean and organize everything. The bays were where the soldiers slept each night.

Let me go back to 1999, because this was the year my twins were born. My wife at that time and I were blessed with amazing fraternal twins, a boy and a girl. Their names are Brittany and Brandon. It was difficult in the beginning trying to raise twins because we needed two of everything, and since they were boy and girl, there was no sharing. We had help at times as well with things they needed from family, but it was a challenge at first — not to mention when I became a drill sergeant. I was gone most of the time working at training soldiers. Somehow by the grace of God we managed it, and they grew up so quickly. It was here that I started missing out on my kids' accomplishments, like walking, riding bikes, and other milestones. Like I said earlier in the book, sacrifices were something I got accustomed to.

Now at this time I had three kids, one boy and two girls. My oldest daughter, Teri, was seven or eight years old and living in North Carolina with her mom. I didn't get chance to see her often, and as time went, we grew more and more apart. It wasn't that I didn't want to see her, but the military had me so busy. Again, I missed so much as she got older, but I was glad to be there during her early age. Sometimes in life all we will ever have is our memory, and then that will be gone one day. I just thank God for the wonderful times with my kids. I never knew what the military was going to bring during my career, but I learned to be flexible with whatever came forth, and man did it ever! Going back to my Army Reserve years, I had eight years under my belt, and now I had five years on active duty.

My kids were so very important to me, and I love them dearly. Now as my drill sergeant duty would come to an end, it was time to move on to another duty station. I had three choices as far as where I could go, and those places were Hawaii, Germany, and Alaska. Of course the best choice that anyone would pick was Hawaii, and of course I did so. I was excited about my next duty assignment and in a hurry to go. At the end of my two-year drill sergeant assignment, there was an option to voluntarily extend for a third year, but I wasn't interested. I chose to accept my assignment and leave before the drill sergeant position became an involuntary third-year assignment. So I received my assignment orders and prepared myself for another permanent change of station, Hawaii.

It was now the year of 2001 and I was headed to paradise: Hawaii. My family at the time was not with me, and as things went on and time went by, we divorced for various reasons. Now again I was in a such a beautiful place without my kids, Teri, Brittany and Brandon. The sacrifices were still a major part of my life, and this would at most times affect my family. Hawaii was where I was about to start a new chapter in my life, but I didn't know that at the time. I would meet new people in a new unit. My family and friends would always want to know, "How was Hawaii? Was it beautiful? How friendly were the people?" They didn't realize that I was still in the Army.

As time went by, I got in the routine of my new unit and everyone I worked with. Remember I was a 13B, a field artillery soldier. The good thing about being in Hawaii was that no matter how much we would train, go to the field, or do other things, we always got three- and four-day weekends for holidays. In Hawaii they called them ADONSA — a day of nonscheduled activities. But let me go back a moment. When I got to Hawaii I was greeted and picked up from the airport by one of my soldiers when I was a drill sergeant. You see, my platoon sergeant in drill sergeant school was her platoon sergeant in Hawaii as well. They both ended up in Hawaii in the same unit again — what a coincidence.

I was often in contact with my former platoon sergeant, knowing she went to Hawaii, so I had let her know I would be coming there as well. She made it possible for my former soldier, Lowanda Matthews, and a couple of other soldiers to pick me up from the airport. It was great being greeted by familiar faces, people I knew. I was so thankful for them helping me get settled in and getting me around places until my car could be shipped from Oklahoma. There was so much to do and see in Hawaii that you needed your own transportation, and I was so glad when mine arrived. Once my vehicle arrived, I started going around to various places and getting myself acclimated. I eventually found a condo not too far from base, Schofield Barracks, located in Oahu, Hawaii.

Now back to my unit. As time went on, we trained and trained. I would get up, leave my home, and drive to work for physical training and then a full work day. At times we would travel to the Big Island, which was called the Island of Hawai'I, to train. This was the largest of the eight major islands in the Hawaiian archipelago. We would pack and load our equipment for about a 45-50 min flight. The training was awesome at Schofield Barracks. Being in an air assault unit, it was looked upon being air assault certified, especially as a non-commissioned officer (NCO). So of course I enrolled in the school, and with some vigorous and intensive training, I earned my air assault wings. That was probably the toughest school I would ever go through besides drill sergeant school.

Time went on and I was still enjoying myself with work and all the ADONSAs we would get until 2004 came. This was the year of my second deployment, in which we were scheduled to deploy to Afghanistan for Operation Enduring Freedom (OEF). I would reflect back on my first deployment to Bosnia back when I was stationed at Fort Hood, Texas, but of course a very different mission. This deployment we were going to combat. As a field artillery unit, that is what our job was, combat. We were to support other units with artillery. I said goodbye to family and friends, not knowing what was going to happen across the waters, but I just knew that I had a praying family and they would be who would get me through whatever was to come forth.

I was deployed for over a year, about thirteen or fourteen months. I saw and experienced some horrific things in Afghanistan. There were so many times I didn't know if I would return back to my loving family. But by the grace of God and a praying family, I would return back to Schofield Barracks, Hawaii. Unfortunately, some of my comrades didn't. My second deployment was completed, and I was glad to be back home. We would have to go through some more training to get us acclimated to our return. You'd be surprised at the things that we would have to get used to again back home. It went from getting comfortable driving to being back with our family. Being deployed for lengthy times in a combat environment did something to my mind and thoughts. Mandatory classes were definitely needed.

So now it was 2005, a new year. I would get married to an amazing woman who was previously in the Army as well. We had met before my deployment, but later it became a relationship. If I can remind you of one of the persons who picked me up from the airport when I arrived to Hawaii, it was she whom I married. Talk about a small world! I won't get into all the details, but there are three sides to this story: my side, her side, and the truth. Her name was Lowanda Matthews at the time. I can still remember how I proposed to her. It was a glass of champagne with a diamond ring at the bottom, and I kneeled down to propose to her. Of course I had to make sure she didn't swallow the ring, but it went as planned and I have no regrets.

As we planned the wedding, we realized that much of our family would not be able to attend due to us being in Hawaii. But what made it so great was the fact we could get married on an island of paradise, despite not having family there. So we decided to get married on one of the many beautiful beaches of Hawaii. We had a few friends there to be a part of our special day. It was the most beautiful day, and as we looked down the beach, we could see other small wedding ceremonies taking place. We got married on the beach and went back to our home and had a reception at the clubhouse by the pool. That was a great day and another new chapter in my life. My wife would eventually get out of the Army because being dual military was a challenge.

We would both start our new lives together and enjoy being married on such a lovely island. Once my wife got out of the Army, she received a government job on the Marine base. Life, work, and now marriage were great again! Hawaii was one of the best places I've lived, and having someone to share it with despite my family not being there was great. I would often reflect back on being deployed and all the things that happened. I missed so much during that deployment in 2004. There were three deaths in my family while I was deployed: my aunt, my first cousin, and one of my grandmothers, and I couldn't make it back home for any of their funerals. That was something that weighed strong on my heart. I wouldn't show my feelings and thoughts much around people. I guess that was called being strong.

We weren't fortunate to have our family at our wedding but we were blessed to have them visit us in Hawaii. I would always tell them now is best time to come because they had a place to stay besides a hotel — our home. So we flew our parents to Hawaii to visit. My wife's sister and brother-in-law came a few days later. It was so much fun, and my wife and I often talked about it. We had a total of nine people in our town home, which made it so much fun because it was all family! I would always joke about the sleeping arrangements. My wife and I went from the air mattress, to the sleeper sofa, to the futon, and finally back to our own bedroom. That is what made it so much fun, staying up all night talking and laughing about old memories and figuring out what we would do next during their visit. Of course my wife always had an agenda of stuff, and the one thing we made sure to do was a luau, or a traditional Hawaiian party.

That was a much-needed break, but after everyone left it was back to work for both of us. Now another year had passed, and it was 2006. We got the news that another deployment was getting ready happen, and this time we were heading to Iraq for Operation Iraqi Freedom (OIF). Now, this deployment was a tough one. Not only was it going to be deployment number three, but I was about to leave my wife before our one-year anniversary. The moment came for us to leave and head to Iraq into another combat zone. Being in Iraq was difficult for me. I knew how to prepare myself to be gone for a while, but I had to adjust to a lot of new things happening in my life and family. It was going to be yet another lengthy deployment, and this one came up quickly, seeing we had just returned from Afghanistan in 2005.

Back when I was a drill sergeant and chose to be stationed in Hawaii, it wasn't a deployment duty station until 2004. I always wondered if I still would have chosen Hawaii knowing I would deploy so much. I arrived in Hawaii in 2001, and it was now 2006 and I was on my second deployment out of Schofield Barracks, Hawaii. The 25th Infantry Division became a rotating deployment duty for us all, artillery and infantry. We arrived in Iraq and started our deployment. Iraq was a different type of mission for us and required multiple jobs for us. I remember one evening standing outside my room with a couple of soldiers and a rocket came in from the enemy and the ground shook from an explosion less than 100 meters from us.

It was then I knew this deployment was going to be a long one. Nevertheless, I dug in deep and focused on my mission and time in Iraq. We were on a one-year deployment, so seeing that I just got back a year ago from doing one, it was going to be tolerable. As you remember, I mentioned we left before my one-year wedding anniversary, and I was looking forward to getting back. There was one evening I had opportunity to talk to my wife and the conversation was great. There was a moment during our conversation where I would pause because of something she had mentioned. She informed me that we were about to be extended another 90 days or so, and in my mind I was thinking, "Three more months! Wow, this is crazy." You see, what made it hard was we had less than sixty days left until we would go back home.

Being a leader and having soldiers whom I was in charge of, I had to keep my focus and stay optimistic. You could see the morale of everyone start to drop, and that was something we couldn't let happen because we were still at war. Unfortunately, during that time we lost a few comrades and had to deal with that moment as well. I saw and experienced so much during my deployments, which at moments I would reflect back on. We got the news from our commanders it was set it stone, the extended ninety days or so. So now not only would I have another three months in combat, but I would miss my one-year anniversary. There were quite a few times that sacrifices were made, and most often, not by choice.

It was now 2007 and we ended up doing almost a seventeen-month deployment. The time went by, and we redeployed back to Schofield Barracks, Hawaii. It was great seeing our family and all the support of our unit once we landed and set foot on the base. I was back home and happy to see my wife. As always, once we finished all the required classes needed after a deployment, we would get some much needed time off. I didn't go home much because being in Hawaii I would have had to fly, and so my wife and I would just enjoy being with one another and visiting some of the other islands. We would explore the islands of Hawai'i, Maui, and Kauai. The most memorable was the black sand beaches in Maui and then driving the winding roads of Hana Highway up to Haleakala National Park. There was so much beauty to see! We also took a trip to Las Vegas with a couple of great friends and celebrated our missed anniversary.

It was now 2008 and time was going by so quickly being on the island. After two deployments there, 2004-05 and 2006-07, little did I know we were about to do a third deployment back to Iraq. By a great surprise and blessing, I came out on the E-8 list for promotion. After talking with the promotion department, I received a message from the Department of Army stating it was time for me to PCS due to me being on the E-8 list. Also at that time my wife, was offered a promotion at her job that was awesome as well, so I had to make a decision. I should also mention my wife was pregnant. The question I was facing was this: Should I stay and deploy again and my wife accept her promotion, or should we leave, not deploy for a third back-to-back deployment, and start somewhere new? After talking with my wife, the choice was easy, especially with us expecting a baby, and so we ended up leaving Hawaii.

As we left Hawaii, we both reflected on all the great moments we had experienced there. All of our family had a chance to visit us there, and we keep those memories near to our hearts. We took some time to visit our family before reporting to my new duty station. I was heading back to the place where I was a drill sergeant, Fort Sill, Oklahoma. My assignment at Fort Sill was as a first sergeant/1SG in a basic training unit. The same place I was a drill sergeant, I would now be a 1SG in charge of drill sergeants. I was excited about my new job and my promotion. The one thing about being in the military is that you never knew where you would end up being stationed during your career. I was now fourteen years in my active duty career and was happy about it.

When we got to my unit and were supposed to start working, my wife went into labor, almost two months early. My wife was transferred to Oklahoma City, Oklahoma, to the Womens Hospital, where our son Braylon was born. Despite his being two months early, there were minimal health issues concerning our son. Once he and my wife were healthy enough, they both was discharged back to Lawton, Oklahoma, the city where the base was located. The funny thing about this is that our son took his first ride on a helicopter from Oklahoma City to Lawton. Being premature and released from the NICU, he had to be flown back to the Lawton, Oklahoma, hospital, where he would stay for a couple more weeks before going home. We got through all this, and it was back to work as usual. My wife and Braylon got stronger, and life was soon back to normal.

My time in Fort Sill was great, and work was great as well. Being there as a first sergeant was much different than being there as a drill sergeant. The hours were much less, and family was greater. Now since we were back closer to our family, they would often come to visit us, especially to see their newest grandchild. Time went on, and going into 2010 I came down on orders to PCS to Korea for a hardship tour, twelve months unaccompanied. This meant I would be going to Korea without my family. Everything I did and every decision I made was for my career and family. With the family part came many sacrifices, and I thank my wife for holding it down during those times! She was definitely a trooper, and, having been in the military herself, taught that to our son.

It was now 2010 and I was about to head to Korea for another one-year separation from my family. As always, I prepared for another move and looked forward to going and returning. I left for South Korea and enjoyed the long flight there reflecting back on my career thus far and family. Once I got there, I was assigned to my unit, the Second Infantry Division at Camp Casey, South Korea. Camp Casey was based in Dongducheon, South Korea, about forty miles north of Seoul, South Korea. Again I was assigned as the headquarters first sergeant. Being close to the Korean Demilitarized Zone (DMZ), we were constantly training, having meetings and alerts, and going to the field to stay ready for a possible North/South Korea War. We were a family in Korea.

I met some awesome brothers in Korea, especially my fellow first sergeants, my battle buddies and my command sergeant major. Like I mentioned, we all became a family away from family. We all had the same thing in common, our families being back home and not with us. Despite the numerous alerts, going to the field and other things, we had moments when we would travel. Korea was a place where there was lots to see and do. Experiencing the culture and food was exciting. Often myself and a couple other first sergeants would take the bus or train to Seoul or to Osan Air Force Base in Songtan, South Korea, to get away and just relax away from the soldiers. Being stationed in Korea I had some good times and some not-so-good times. The best thing was learning the Korean culture and being a part of it.

Now going into 2011 I had reached my one-year obligation and was looking forward to being back with my family. But again, there was a stop movement order for various reasons, so I ended up doing another three months.

After finishing my time in Korea I was back in the wonderful United States of America. I returned to Fort Sill, Oklahoma, to out-process and move to my new assignment at Fort Campbell, Kentucky. So it was 2011 and I was now in Fort Campbell. This Army installation is located astride the Kentucky-Tennessee border between Hopkinsville, Kentucky, and Clarksville, Tennessee. Fort Campbell is known as the home to the 101st Airborne Division and the 160th Special Operations Aviation Regiment. So my already being air assault certified made it a great assignment. My family and I looked forward to being stationed in this area; it was a change of scenery, so to speak!

Once we got settled in, it was back to work as usual! I was again assigned as the battalion first sergeant. We were always busy training and in the field a lot. When we did get time off and on weekends, my family and I would hit the road and sight-see. One great place we would always go was Nashville, Tennessee, which was about one hour from us, so it was a nice drive to go and come back. It was about spending time with family again, since I was just returning from Korea. The great thing about Fort Campbell was the fact that we were on the border of Kentucky and Tennessee. We could come out the main gate and make a left to the Kentucky side or a right to Tennessee. We enjoyed the time there and made the best of it. I would say it was probably number two for best assignments for me, with Hawaii being number one, of course!

We were now in 2012 and everything was going great! The family and I had adjusted with work and made incredible friends. But wait, it was time for another combat deployment back to Afghanistan. I was not looking forward to it at all, but I knew Fort Campbell was a rapid deployment assignment. Seeing this was going to be my fifth deployment, I some knew this would be it for me. I was tired of deploying and not knowing if I was going to return or not. This deployment was going to be different than all my previous ones.

The hardest thing about this deployment was my youngest son Braylon was only four years old and for some reason it affected me a lot. But I knew my wife was a trooper when it came to me leaving, and that helped a lot. We left for Afghanistan and ended up doing about fourteen months. This was a tough deployment for me and the unit, and some didn't make it back home! Once we made it back home, we took a much-needed leave for vacation. I looked forward to being back and seeing my family! This was probably the most memorable moment of me returning from a deployment because the look I got from my four-year-old son when he was in my arms is unforgettable! I did a little over two years at Fort Campbell, and now was time for my last move.

Now 2013, we were on our way to Fort Valley, Georgia, where I would take an assignment as the senior military science instructor in the Reserve Officer Training Corps (ROTC) program at the Fort Valley State University. I was excited about this assignment, and it was something that I asked for. I knew I was at the end of my Army career and wanted to finish with something that didn't require deploying and was not so fast paced. ROTC is a program offered at colleges and universities that prepares young adults to become officers in the U.S. military. It was an awesome job to have. The greatest thing about it was teaching and mentoring the young college kids while also sharing my twenty-six years of military experience with them.

I also met some great people, friends and coworkers. This was a great assignment and definitely the perfect one to end out my military career. It was something I enjoyed doing, and we had a great team as well. The commencement ceremonies were the best! Just seeing the young cadets being commissioned brought a huge appreciation for what I did, similar to when I was a drill sergeant. The senior military science instructor in the ROTC program was same as the first sergeant role. I really enjoyed my job! But as all good things come to an end, it was time for my military career to come to an end. I had a command sergeant major who would always tell me, "You'll know when it's time to retire, first sergeant." That day came when I knew it was time. The moment when it wasn't fun anymore was the time to end and with no regrets! I had none!

It was now 2015, the end of my military career. Like I

mentioned before, I had no regrets, and retiring was the best thing to do. The military taught me a whole lot from the time I started up to the last day I served. It taught me loyalty, duty, respect, selfless service, honor, integrity, and personal courage. Those are the seven Army values. That was what being a soldier was all about: living and modeling each core value every day, no matter the situation. Wearing the uniform exemplified each value and was a proud moment. Retiring was a simple decision to make, and I left with no animosity or no regrets. So October 1, 2015, I officially retired from the U.S. Army.

I remember during my retirement ceremony I made an announcement that was surprising to my wife. I talked about lots of things, but the one thing I mentioned was going to culinary school. I didn't want to do anything else but something quite different in my life. I hadn't talked with my wife about at all. Also, I had my Post 9/11 GI Bill to use toward school, and so I did so. No one at my retirement ceremony knew how to respond, but their support was there, including my wife's and family's. I always was fascinated with cooking, but my wife did all the cooking, and with her being from Baton Rouge, she knew exactly what she was doing. So I guess watching all the cooking and food shows on TV made me interested in learning more.

Lifetime Military Experiences

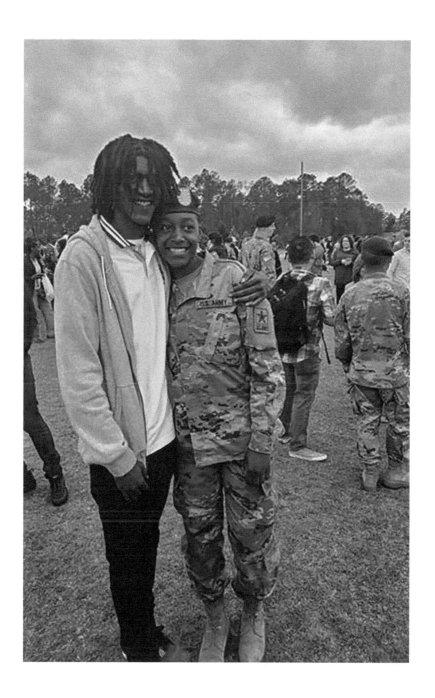

STORY FOUR

Chef Life (Finding My Gift)

I retired October 1, 2015, and ten days later I enrolled in the Culinary Arts Program at Helms College in Macon, Georgia. Now as I look back I realize that I was about to embark on another journey. My first was going to college, thenext was the military, and now was the culinary industry. I was excited about culinary school, and once started, I realized that the one thing that my military career had helped me with was discipline. Culinary school was disciplined and time-sensitive school. There was a uniform we had to wear each day, an inspection we had to go through each morning before class started, and responsibility we had to learn throughout the program. So this part came easy for me to lock in and do a great job at.

As time went by in school, I found myself being seen as a leader, a mentor, and a professional. Each day I went to class was honestly a great learning experience. Most people would think that culinary arts school was about cooking but actually it wasn't. We were taught the business side to include management, cost and control, trademarking, and the like. We also learned the dietitian and nutrition part of the industry. There were tests on everything and major projects as well.

I really enjoyed going to class and learning so much about cooking and food. I challenged myself to do great and found myself on the dean's list, then making the president's list. All the hard work, commitment, and dedication I put in resulted in my graduating at the top of my class.

I had some amazing instructors who not only taught me but were mentors as well. Most of them became my friends and still are at this present time. An amazing thing happened after I graduated. I was asked if would consider coming back to be a teaching assistant (TA). Of course, throughout my military career, that was all I did, mentor and teach, and so being a culinary arts instructor was right up my alley. So I went back to the college to help teach young students all about the culinary arts world. It was great mentoring and teaching the students, and at the same time it was making me more knowledgeable. Also, while working alongside the other chef instructors, I increased my knowledge of the culinary industry. It was an amazing time in my life, and I enjoyed every moment.

I recall as a student competing in a contest against other teams from both campuses, Macon and Augusta, Georgia. We had teams of three people, and my team won first place. As I continued teaching, I decided to start my own business sharing with others my culinary skills and gifts. So my wife and I started our private chef services business in Warner Robins, Georgia, also known as the Middle Georgia area around here. As I continued teaching, I started introducing my business to people, and before long I had clients wanting my service. It became so much that I had to make the decision to stop teaching and focus on my business, so that is what I did. Nothing I've done there was ever a regret. I believe each step was just to make me better at each journey in life. Now there was what you call "a vision" in sight.

In 2016, my business had started to pick up. My wife named the business Blessed and Highly Flavored Cuisine – Private Chef Services. We decided to name it that because as Christians we felt we were very blessed and of course the food was very flavored. My type of food is a Cajun-Southern cuisine. My wife being from Baton Rouge and my being from North Carolina, we brought in her Cajun flavors and my Southern flavors together. It was a hit with all our clients! You see there is a scripture in the Bible about vision, Habakkuk 2:2: "Write the vision; make it plain on tablets, that he may run who reads it." That's how the title of this book, Vision Your Route and Run It, came into mind! We all have a vision in life, though we may not notice it. But it's not IF you see it, but rather WHEN you see it, that you must run your route.

I never imagined me starting a career as a chef in this huge culinary arts world. It also amazed my family and friends at how much it grew on me and my desire to do so much more with it. I know the answer to how and why it became so desirable and obtainable was because of my leap of faith. The Bible tells us that all we need is to have faith the size of a mustard seed. I took a huge leap not knowing what to expect and no money coming in besides a retirement check. But what I knew was that whatever you give to God and ask for in prayer, His direction and guidance you will receive, and no one can take that from you. I come from a spiritual family and prayer is a must! That was also one of the reasons we decided to make Kathleen, Georgia, our home, because of great friends and our church home.

Being a chef here has been enormously rewarding. Most people know me very well and sometimes refer to me as "Deacon Chef Scottie." Oh yes, I am also an ordained deacon in my church. Most of my clients don't know that, but we are always focusing on the food. Everyone who follows me would probably know, but I'm just blessed to have the support! The best part about being a private chef is the fact that I go into amazing people's homes and take over their kitchen. I bring gourmet dinning experiences to the comfort of their homes. My joy comes from the expressions on each face and the compliments given afterwards. I guess you can say that's a huge reason why I love doing it. I would always tell my students that getting into this industry while at a young age is great, even though I started this career late in my life — but better late than never for doing something you enjoy.

Moving forward to 2019, my client list grew tremendously. I would often be asked how long have I been cooking or if I cooked in the military? They would be shocked when I answered I had been cooking only a few years, and no, I didn't cook in the military. My business was going well and we were having fun providing my services as a private chef. I mostly catered to small parties (anniversaries, birthdays, couples' dinners, staff meetings, etc.). I think what made us a hit with clients was the fact we brought fine dining cuisine into the comfort of people's homes. We provided two- to four-course meals to our clients. My joy came from the expressions on everyone's faces once they tasted the food.

The unique thing about our business was that my wife and I were teammates. I focused on the food, and she focused on the decorative side, making it intimate for our clients. We brought the restaurant to people's homes and prepared a gourmet dinner for them. Dinner would be a romantic candlelight dinner with some jazz, wine, and the aroma of the food in the air. I would always tell people that they didn't have to find a parking spot or wait to be seated due to reservations. All they needed to do was just relax and enjoy the evening. I would enjoy great conversations with my clients while cooking the food. I would hear light music and laughter in the background while louder conversations were taking place at the bar and kitchen area.

I didn't know how much I would love being a chef when I first started. I didn't know the passion I would have coming into this industry. But what I did was take that passion and turn into a presentation. Everything I did was with a spirit of excellence. I had the vision and along with the vision I had to run my route.

My passion was in my presentation and my presentation was in my passion. Those words are what I lived by and modeled everyday. I would look at food as an art when plating it. You see, painters would paint art on how they saw things on canvas, and as a chef I would treat food as art and plate it like a picture as I would see it. I would always remember growing up and also with my kids that we all eat with our eyes! A nice plated dish would be appealing to the eyes and would be more enjoyable than one that was not. I fell in love with cooking and being able to share with others my passion of cooking. I remember that old saying, "Grandma cooked with love." Now I know what that means!

Being a chef was amazing, and I enjoyed getting in the kitchen thinking of different ways to put a twist on old family dishes. It was the part of being creative when working with different types of food. The experimenting with various herbs and seasonings and then pairing them with foods was the best. Some came out great and some not that well, but figuring it out before serving to my clients was a plus. Like I mentioned before, people always thought I cooked in the Army, but little did they know I only started cooking when I retired and finished culinary school. My wife being from Baton Rouge was our family's cook, and her food was amazing! She will say to this day that, she had a part with my great seasoning of food. I guess I can accept that. She was the taste tester of every dish I made.

As time went on, I would find myself in the kitchen

almost the whole day! I would reflect back on when my grandmother would wake up on a Sunday morning and prepare a full dinner before we all would leave for church. I never knew how she did it, but we always enjoyed our Sunday dinner. I finally realized that it was the prepping that was important and made life much easier when preparing for a dinner. In the culinary arts world, we call it "mise en place," everything in its place. It was kind of funny because I would relate that to my wife all the time when we prepared for a long trip or vacation. She was horrible when it came to packing; always the night before leaving was when she started, and that resulted in a long night up before going to bed and resting.

I was enjoying all the great things that were happening with my business but wanted to do something out of my comfort zone. After seeing a post from a celebrity chef on social media about a Georgia Seafood Festival Cooking Competition, I submitted my information and bio. This was going to be the first ever seafood festival competition in Atlanta, Georgia. I'm not really a chef who likes to compete, but I wanted to prove something to myself, and that's why I decided to submit my packet. After several weeks I heard back and was notified that I would be one of the four chefs to compete in this competition. I was excited to be selected and especially to represent Warner Robins, Georgia. The competition date was November 9, 2019, and it was held at the Battery Atlanta, where the Atlanta Braves play. It was going to be held outside in the open area.

Georgia is known for great seafood, and this festival was going to showcase it along with a cooking competition. I was so excited and nervous to be competing, but the excitement outweighed the nervousness. The exciting part of the competition was the fact it was a blind-box type of competition, meaning we didn't know what the ingredients were, except all three rounds would consist of an unknown seafood. So the family and I left for Atlanta the day before the event. I wanted to just get there and check out everything then relax.

We got to the hotel and checked in at the front desk. I knew God's favor was already happening because the room they gave us was way on the other side. After my wife explained to the nice lady at the front desk that I was competing in the festival, she reassigned us a deluxe room with the whole view of where the competition was taking place. The view overlooked parts of the stadium and all of the yard. We went to get something to eat and then came back to the room and just looked as the set-up was taken place. After about an hour I decided to go to bed and get my thoughts together and relax. My wife and other friends would ask me during that evening if I was nervous, but for some reason I wasn't.I slept like a brand-new baby and woke up the next morning restedand full of energy.

It was competition day and a very chilly morning as well. I got up, got dressed, and had a cup of coffee. I then went downstairs to the yard to check in the competition and get my location area for the competition. I settled in my spot and began to get everything in place as I waited on my sous chefs to arrive. It was a very chilly morning with the wind blowing, but despite all that, it was a beautiful day. The set-up was really nice and everything we needed was being put in place. The staff was doing their last-minute set-ups and making sure we had everything we needed. It was four of us chefs competing. As the time got closer I could see the crowd growing, and I could feel the excitement growing even more. My sous chefs arrived and we were good to go.

The greatest moment was seeing my friends, family, and church members there to support and cheer me on. My parents and sister couldn't make it, but having my aunt, uncle, and cousin and her husband attend was awesome. Of course my wife and son were there as always to cheer me on. The favor of God was definitely there that day! It was quite amazing having my own cheering section in the corner shouting my name. I feel everything was orchestrated by God because it all fell in place with the weather, environment, chemistry, excitement, calmness, and even my area of work. If you believe in God, you would understand exactly what I was talking about and experiencing that day.

So now it was getting close to start time of the competition, and everyone was excited. I could hear the laughter and conversations and feel the energy that was present. I had a very nice lady who approached me and ask who I was. She told me that I was her favorite and I was going to win it all. She also asked to take a picture with me and that she was a fan. That was awesome, because for one thing I had never met this lady before until that moment. I guess she could feel all the energy that was coming from the section of the crowd and all my supporters. Surprisingly, that was only the beginning of what was about to take place. I had my fan club section in my corner, and they made sure to make themselves known and who they were cheering for. When I say the energy was crazy, that is an understatement.

Now as the host began to make his announcement that the competition was about to begin, he introduced the four of us chefs and our teams. This competition was a huge one, and the local news stations, journalists, professional photographers, and video cameras made it a highly visible event. We were in the big City of Atlanta, Georgia. There were hundreds and hundreds of spectators there to watch and enjoy great food, drinks, and music. It was now time for the competition to start and all the rules were given out to each of us. As we all met each other we embraced one another with smile, telling each other to have fun and good luck. During all this I was calm and in my element. My strategy was to treat it like I normally would with my clients. I told my team, "Let's do what we love and have passion for and have fun. Everything else will fall in place."

The rules were as follows. We had three rounds of cooking with each being a mystery protein of seafood. We had an outdoor pantry to select all our veggies and other stuff needed to finish and accompany the dish. There were four celebrity judges who we had to prepare dishes for in the thirty-minute rounds. The total points from all three rounds would be tallied up, with 100 being the maximum number of points that could be given each round. There were also bonus points that could be given if desired. We had total of thirty minutes per round to prepare four complete dishes to the judges. When you think about it, thirty minutes go by so quickly! I and my team were ready to get this thing going. As we got our first-round mystery protein, which was shrimp and sausage, I had to decide on what I was going to prepare.

I decided to prepare one of my signature dishes, which was a succotash, but I made a shrimp-and-sausage succotash. My sous chefs and I went to the pantry that was provided and got all the items needed to accompany the protein. We grabbed everything and came back to our food station and began to prepare the dish. I assigned both of them different areas to focus on, and we would put it all together at the end. The dish consisted of various bell peppers, onions, corn, herbs, and the secret protein, shrimp and sausage. As the time was winding down and we got it all put together, I plated it to be ready to serve. I think we had less than 15 seconds remaining once done. We took it to the wire, so to speak. I was the last person to present to the judges so I had to make sure it stayed hot. I put the four plates inside the grill and when I presented to the judges, I made sure to tell them to be cautious of the

HOT plates. As I explained my dish to the judges, they all gave me great feedback. I received 100s across the board. This was a great start for the first round, and it gave us much more fuel to the fire. We were ready to see what was in store for the second round.

Now it was on to the second round, and the secret ingredients were salmon and tequila. These were two ingredients that I was excited about using, especially together. Again, my sous chefs and I huddled up and came up with a game plan. I decided to do a pan-seared salmon with a roasted red bell pepper tequila cream sauce. We got what we needed from the pantry to again accompany the salmon and the tequila. I handled the salmon as my sous chefs roasted the peppers to start the sauce. I can say I'm close to perfection when cooking salmon, and that was what I had my mind focused on. We again put it all together, and I plated it to so well. The salmon was pan-seared in duck fat and butter with Cajun seasoning. It was finished with a nice creamy roasted pepper sauce with a touch of tequila and garnished with some fried onions. That was my sous chef's idea! I was third in line to present. Once again when presenting to the judges, they each had great feedback. I recall one asking for the name of the dish and saying this could very well be a $10,000 dish.

Going into the third and final round, we had continued to lead the way in scoring. We were tied with one of the other chefs going into the final round, so we knew we had to bring it, and bring it is what we did. It was now the final round, and the secret ingredients were crawfish and lobster tails. Now again, this was another one of my favorites to prepare. I had an idea to utilize pasta and add a touch of squid ink to it. This would give my dish a taste of the ocean along with the lobster and crawfish. We gathered everything needed for my final dish. I decided to do a crawfish cream sauce with grilled lobster tails and squid ink pasta. The flavors were on point and just waiting to hit the judges' palates. I and my sous chefs prepared this dish with so much passion. I mean, every detail was done precisely; it needed to be in order to come out on top. As the time came to an end, I plated four dishes for the judges. We took the dishes to the judges, and I explained the dish distinctly. Once again the judges had nothing but great things to say, and I walked away with a huge smile on my face. It was finally over with, and now we would just have to wait for the announcement of the winner.

I thanked my sous chefs for the great job they did and for being awesome team players. As we patiently waited for the judges to tally up their scores and for the host to announce, I just thanked God for the opportunity of being in place and being by my side during the entire competition. The host got our attention to let us know that the final scores were in. The four of us chefs came to the center and stood side by side. The results were announced by fourth place and up. As the fourth and third place was announced, I was still standing in the top two. As I mentioned earlier, I was tied for first place going into the final round, so it wasn't a surprise I was left. It was announced that the winner had won by nine points, and that was huge!

As I looked out into the crowd I heard this: "The winner of the 2019 Georgia Seafood Competition is Chef Scottie Johnson!" I was so happy and had a feeling that came upon me like no other. I immediately thanked God and gave him all the glory! I could hear the loud chants and the hand-clapping and yelling for joy from all the crowd, especially my wonderful family, friends, and church members! My sous chefs and I slapped hands and gave each other a great big hug. It was a great day and one that I will never forget! My wife and son ran to me and we all hugged and kissed! The atmosphere was filled with so much excitement and joy. The love and appreciation shown was so genuine. I was so thankful for everything that took place that day. I was truly grateful to God for what took place!

The lights from the flashes of cameras and video recordings were everywhere. I took pictures with all the hosts, judges, family, and friends. I also received my Golden Ticket for the World Food Championship (WFC). Along with that, I was to get a trophy knife. The material prizes were great, but what was more important too me is the fact I was the 2019 Georgia Seafood Festival champion, the award-winning chef. I would have to say that this award was the best because it was something that I wanted to prove and challenge myself. I'm not a huge fan of competitions, but this one was personal to me! I set my mind on doing something, and I did it with passion, a spirit of excellence, and confidence. At the end of it all, I always say "To God be the glory!"

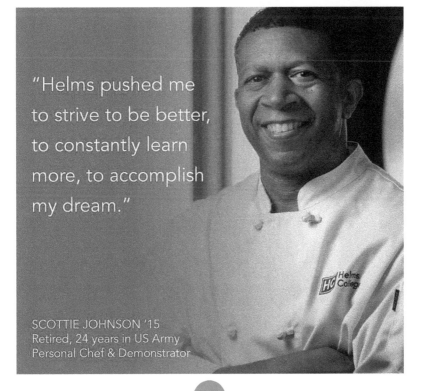

"Helms pushed me to strive to be better, to constantly learn more, to accomplish my dream."

SCOTTIE JOHNSON '15
Retired, 24 years in US Army
Personal Chef & Demonstrator

My career as a private chef continued to take off and grow. I started getting more and more exposure. I've had consistent appearances and been featured by 41 NBC News at Daybreak, 13 WMAZ, the Macon Telegraph, the Houston Home Journal, Georgia Magazine, Real Talk TV WDIG, T.E.A. Time Louddmouth Radio, Voyage ATL Magazine and many more. I often look back at the day I decided to attend culinary arts school, and I realize that I didn't understand the magnitude that would take place. Everything was great because it was something that I had a passion in doing. Life is about choices, dreams and visions. The most difficult part is determining what our choices are and picking the right ones. We will sometimes make the wrong choices, but that's when we learn and grow. God has created us in his own image, and we must strive for perfection in all we do. I will say it again — our visions determine our direction, and without one we will never move forward.

I've grown now into a great chef. My accomplishments are very important at this moment in my life and career. I really enjoy cooking and sharing with others my passion of cooking great dishes. But now I have also taken on other tasks in my career. The COVID-19 pandemic hit hard around March 2020, and pretty much shut everything down, along with doing private events. So my wife and I decided to start quarantine live cooking on Facebook. I didn't realize it would take off like it did, but the viewers were loving every moment. It not only taught them how to prepare dishes but provided entertainment. We went live every week and the viewers grew and grew. I enjoyed the cooking, talking, and teaching on social media. It became something that everyone would look forward to each week. I then was approached about doing an online streaming cooking show. So I accepted, and we begin shooting nine episodes with others to come.

I am excited to share my story and all my accomplishments in this book. I hope that as you read this book, you have come to know who I am and my journey to becoming a great chef. Again, this book is written to share not only great recipes but also a story. I never envisioned or thought about becoming a chef as a kid growing up, but I did enjoy food, of course. I became a chef four years ago at the age of 47, and I have enjoyed every moment. I decided now at the age of fifty-one to write this book about my path to where I am today and how I got here. With the support of family, friends and others, I was able to write and share with you. Remember, it is never too late to "See Your Route and Run it"! God bless each and every one of you who took the time to read, and I hope you enjoy the fantastic recipes.

BONUS

Recipes From Chef Scottie's Kitchen to Yours

BACON CREAM SAUCE

Ingredients

- 3 strips of bacon, cut into bits, cooked with the bacon fat reserved
- 1 tablespoon of chopped shallots or onions
- 2 cloves of garlic minced
- 3/4 cup of good drinking white wine
- 1/4 cup of chicken stock
- 3/4 cup of heavy cream
- 1/2 cup of grated Parmesan cheese, if desired
- sea salt and fresh black pepper to taste
- Cajun seasoning
- basil, fresh chopped

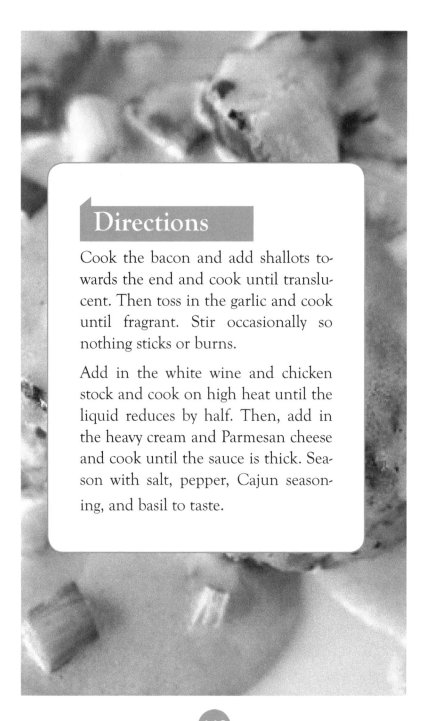

Directions

Cook the bacon and add shallots towards the end and cook until translucent. Then toss in the garlic and cook until fragrant. Stir occasionally so nothing sticks or burns.

Add in the white wine and chicken stock and cook on high heat until the liquid reduces by half. Then, add in the heavy cream and Parmesan cheese and cook until the sauce is thick. Season with salt, pepper, Cajun seasoning, and basil to taste.

MUSTARD VINAIGRETTE

Ingredients

- 2-3 tablespoons mustard
- 1/2 c vinegar
- sea salt
- pinch of brown sugar
- fresh black pepper
- 1 1/2 c olive oil

Directions

Mix all ingredients together; then add olive oil while continuously mixing until blended well.

CRAWFISH CREAM SAUCE

Ingredients

- 4 tablespoons butter
- 2 tablespoons flour
- 12 ounces heavy cream (room temperature or warm); add more if needed
- 1 teaspoon Cajun seasoning
- 1 teaspoon Creole seasoning
- 1/4 teaspoon cayenne pepper
- 1 teaspoon blackening seasoning
- black pepper, to taste
- sea salt, to taste
- 1 teaspoon smoked paprika
- 1 teaspoon lemon juice
- 2 tablespoons white wine
- 8 ounces crawfish tail meat
- chopped parsley, fresh

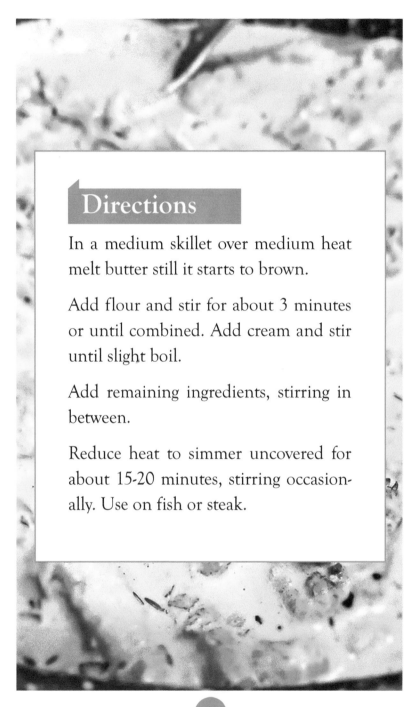

Directions

In a medium skillet over medium heat melt butter still it starts to brown.

Add flour and stir for about 3 minutes or until combined. Add cream and stir until slight boil.

Add remaining ingredients, stirring in between.

Reduce heat to simmer uncovered for about 15-20 minutes, stirring occasionally. Use on fish or steak.

REMOULADE SAUCE

Ingredients

- 1 cup mayonnaise
- 2 tablespoons Dijon mustard
- 1 tablespoon freshly squeezed lemon juice
- 1 tablespoon finely chopped flat-leaf parsley
- 1 tablespoon hot sauce
- 1-2 cloves garlic, minced
- 1 teaspoon Worcestershire sauce
- 1 teaspoon paprika
- 1/4 teaspoon sea salt
- 1/4 teaspoon Cajun seasoning
- 1/8 teaspoon cayenne pepper

Directions

In a small bowl, mix together mayonnaise, Dijon mustard, lemon juice, parsley, hot sauce, garlic, Worcestershire sauce, paprika, Cajun seasoning, salt, and cayenne pepper. Let sit for 1 hour for flavors to combine, then serve or cover and store in the refrigerator.

SPICY ORANGE RUM SAUCE

Ingredients

- 1/2 cup honey
- 1 teaspoon lime juice
- 3 tablespoons spiced rum
- 1 teaspoon grated orange zest
- 1 tablespoon orange juice
- 1 teaspoon grated fresh ginger
- sea salt, to taste
- fresh black pepper, to taste
- cayenne pepper, dash
- 1 teaspoon cornstarch

Directions

Mix together the honey, lime juice, spiced rum, orange zest, orange juice, ginger, salt, black pepper, cayenne, and cornstarch in a large bowl until the glaze is smooth and the cornstarch is thoroughly blended with the rest of the ingredients.

PEACH BOURBON JAM

Ingredients

- 4 fresh peeled peaches finely chopped or peach preserves
- 1-1/2 cups packed brown sugar
- 1 tablespoon lemon juice
- 3 tablespoons bourbon or whiskey
- 1 tablespoon pomegranate molasses
- 1/2 cup bacon, chopped
- pinch of crushed red pepper
- 1/4 teaspoon Creole season
- Sea salt
- smoked black pepper to taste
- 1 teaspoon apple cider vinegar

Directions

1. Chop bacon into pieces and cook until brown.

2. Drain and set aside.

3. In a large saucepan, combine peaches, sugars and lemon juice; bring to a boil. Reduce heat; simmer, uncovered, until mixture is thick, about 30 minutes. Remove from heat. Stir in bourbon.

4. Add bacon to the jam.

CREAMY SAFFRON SAUCE

Ingredients

- 1 tablespoon olive oil
- 1 shallot minced
- 1 garlic clove minced
- 3/4 cup heavy cream
- 1/2 cup white wine
- 1/2 teaspoon saffron
- sea salt, to taste
- freshly ground black pepper, to taste
- 1 teaspoon Cajun seasoning
- 2 tablespoons curly parsley fresh, chopped

Directions

In the same pan, on medium heat, saute the shallot and garlic until shallot is translucent. Deglaze with wine. Scrape up the little bits and continue to cook until most of the wine has evaporated. Add the cream, saffron, and seasoning. Cook sauce on low for about 5-10 minutes or until nappe consistency.

PORT WINE SAUCE

Ingredients

- 1 teaspoon olive oil
- 1/4 cup minced shallots
- 1 tablespoon minced garlic
- 1 teaspoon salt
- 1 teaspoon freshly ground black pepper
- 2 teaspoons sugar
- 1 cup port wine
- 3 cups brown chicken stock

Directions

Heat oil in a large saucepan over high heat. Add shallots, garlic, salt, and pepper, and saute for 1 minute. Stir in sugar and port, bring to a boil, and cook for 3 minutes. Stir in stock and cook over high heat, for about 20 minutes, until reduced and thick enough to coat the back of a spoon (nappe). Remove from heat.

Sauce can be used immediately or covered and refrigerated for up to three days. Reheat before serving.

GORGONZOLA CREAM SAUCE

Ingredients

- 1 tablespoon butter
- 1 shallot, minced
- 1 cup heavy cream
- 1 tsp Cajun season
- pinch of cayenne pepper
- 1/4 pound Gorgonzola
- Sea salt, to taste
- freshly ground black pepper, to taste

Directions

Heat a medium-sized saucepan over medium heat. Add butter to melt. Saute shallots until tender. Add the heavy cream and let reduce by half. Turn heat to low, add the Gorgonzola, and stir until it melts. Season, to taste, using all seasoning.

GRAND MARNIER SAUCE

Ingredients

- 2 egg yolks
- 1/3 cup sugar
- 2 teaspoons flour
- 1 cup milk
- 1/2 cup heavy cream
- 1 to 2 tablespoon Grand Marnier
- 1 tablespoon orange liqueur
- 1 tablespoon vanilla

Directions

Beat egg yolks, sugar and flour with a mixer until lightly bright color.

In a medium saucepan, heat milk and cream until bubbly around the edges.

Beat into yolk mixture.

Transfer to saucepan, and cook gently over low heat, stirring constantly, until thickened.

Stir in the alcohol.

Serve warm or cold.

SPICY TARTAR SAUCE

Ingredients

- 1/2 cup mayonnaise
- 2 tablespoons sweet relish
- 1 tablespoon Champagne or white wine vinegar
- 1 teaspoon Dijon mustard
- sea salt, to taste
- freshly ground black pepper, to taste
- cayenne pepper, to taste
- cajun season, to taste
- Old Bay seasoning, to taste

Directions

Mix all ingredients together until incorporated

SAMBUCA COCKTAIL SAUCE

Ingredients

- - 1/2 cup ketchup
- - 1/4 cup Sambuca
- - 2 tablespoons horseradish or to taste
- - 1 tablespoon lemon juice
- - 1 teaspoon preferred hot sauce
- - 1 teaspoon Worcestershire sauce

Directions

Mix all ingredients together until incorporated. Chill and enjoy.

CREAMY SUN-DRIED TOMATO SAUCE

Ingredients

- 1 tablespoon butter
- 2 1/2 tablespoons olive oil
- sea salt, to taste
- freshly ground black pepper
- 3 tablespoons finely chopped shallot or yellow onion
- 2 cloves garlic, minced
- 1 1/3 cups chicken broth
- 1/2 cup sun-dried tomato, finely chopped
- 1/4 cup heavy cream
- 1/3 cup finely shredded parmesan cheese
- 3 tablespoons chopped fresh basil

Directions

Heat 1 tablespoon olive oil in skillet. Add shallots and saute until nearly soft, about 3 minutes. Add garlic and saute 1 minute longer.

Pour in 1 1/3 cups chicken broth, while scraping bottom to release browned pieces.

Stir in sun-dried tomatoes, season sauce with salt and pepper to taste.

Bring to slight boil and allow to simmer 1 minute, stirring constantly. Add in cream and parmesan, stirring until parmesan has melted. Enjoy

CREAMY LEMON CAPER SAUCE

Ingredients

- 1 tablespoon olive oil
- 4 medium garlic cloves minced
- 1/3 cup dry white wine
- 1 cup chicken stock/ broth
- 3 tablespoons fresh lemon juice
- 4 tablespoons rinsed and drained capers
- 1/2 cup heavy cream
- 3 tablespoons butter

Directions

Add 1 tablespoon butter to pan and melt. Add the garlic and sauté until fragrant. Add wine and bring to a boil, scraping any bits from bottom of pan. Cook until almost evaporated, stirring occasionally. Add 3/4 cup stock/broth to the pan along with the lemon juice; bring to a boil and cook for a further minute.

Cook for 1 minute or until slightly thickened. Stir in the cream and remove from heat. Add remaining butter, and finish with the capers.

BEURRE BLANC

Ingredients

- 1/4 cup dry white wine
- 1/4 cup sherry vinegar
- 2 tablespoons finely chopped shallot
- 1/3 cup heavy cream
- 1/4 teaspoon salt
- 1/8 teaspoon white pepper, or to taste
- 2 sticks (1 cup) butter, cut into pieces and chilled

Directions

Boil wine, vinegar, and shallot in saucepan over medium heat until liquid is slightly thick and reduced to 2 to 3 tablespoons. Add cream, salt, and pepper, and boil 1 minute. Reduce heat to low and add a few tablespoons butter, whisking constantly. Add remaining butter a few pieces at a time, whisking constantly and adding new pieces before previous ones have completely liquidfied, lifting pan from heat occasionally to cool mixture.

Remove from heat, then season to taste with salt and pepper. Discard shallots if not wanted by pouring sauce through a mesh strainer into a bowl while pressing.

OLIVE OIL HERB MIX

- 1 tablespoon minced garlic
- 1 tablespoon fresh rosemary, finely chopped
- 1 tablespoon dried oregano
- 2 teaspoons fresh basil
- 1 teaspoon crushed red pepper flakes
- 1/2 teaspoon sea salt
- 1/2 teaspoon coarsely ground pepper
- 1/2 teaspoon Cajun or Creole seasoning
- 1/4 teaspoon lemon pepper

Directions

Mix all ingredients together until incorporated. Enjoy.

CHICKEN DRY RUB

Ingredients

- 1/2 tablespoon Cayenne pepper
- 1/2 tablespoon pepper
- 1 tablespoon paprika
- 1 tablespoon chili powder
- 2 tablespoons salt
- 1 tablespoon garlic powder
- 1/2 tablespoon Old Bay seasoning
- 1 tablespoon garlic salt
- 1/4 cup brown sugar

Directions

Mix all ingredients together and store in close container until ready to use.

HONEY MANGO SALSA

Ingredients

- 2 ripe mangos, diced (canned mangos, if desired)
- 1 medium red bell pepper, diced
- 1 medium yellow bell pepper, diced
- 1/2 cup chopped red onion
- 1/4 cup fresh cilantro, chopped (if desired)
- 1 jalapeño, seeded and chopped
- 1 large lime, juiced
- salt, to taste
- 1-2 tablespoons honey

Directions

In a bowl, combine the prepared mango, bell pepper, onion, cilantro, and jalapeño. Add honey and the juice of lime and mix well. Season to taste with salt. Let the salsa rest for 10 minutes or longer.

PIMENTO CHEESE DEVILED EGGS

Ingredients

- 12 eggs
- green onions
- 1/4 cup mayonnaise
- Creole mustard
- pimiento peppers, drained
- 1 cup sharp cheddar
- cream cheese, half
- sour cream
- pepper
- salt
- pickled relish
- hot sauce
- paprika
- seasoned bread crumbs or buttered crackers, crumbled

Directions

Blend all in food processor. Fold in pimento peppers. Garnish with bread crumbs, green onions and paprika.

SMOKY DEVILED EGGS

Ingredients

- 12 hard-boiled eggs, peeled
- 1/2 cup mayonnaise
- 1/4 cup creme fraiche
- 1 tablespoon Dijon mustard
- 1 teaspoon granulated onion powder
- 1 teaspoon granulated garlic powder
- 1 teaspoon sea salt
- 1 teaspoon fresh black pepper
- 1 teaspoon Creole seasoning
- 2 teaspoons sweet relish
- 1 teaspoon smoked paprika, plus more for dusting

Directions

Fill pot with water and place eggs inside and bring to a boil. Let boil for about 9 minutes; then remove from heat and cover. Let sit for another 4 minutes. Remove eggs and place in ice water to shock and stop the cooking process. Peel and slice each hard-boiled egg in half lengthwise. Scoop the egg yolks into a medium bowl and mash with a fork. Add the mayonnaise, mustard, and paprika and stir together until completely combined; season with salt, pepper, and all other seasoning. Transfer the mixture to a piping bag and refrigerate until ready to use.

When ready to serve, pipe some of the yolk mixture into each egg white and dust with a little paprika.

FRIED GREEN TOMATOES

Ingredients

- 4 large green tomatoes
- 2 eggs
- 1/2 cup milk
- 1-2 tablespoons hot sauce
- 1 cup all-purpose flour
- 1/2 cup cornmeal
- 1/2 cup bread crumbs, seasoned
- 2 teaspoons sea salt
- 1 teaspoon Cajun seasoning
- 1 teaspoon Creole seasoning
- 1/4 teaspoon fresh black pepper
- canola oil, for frying

Directions

Slice tomatoes 1/2 inch thick. Discard the ends.

Whisk eggs, milk, and hot sauce together in a bowl. Scoop flour onto a plate. Mix cornmeal, bread crumbs, and all seasoning on another plate. Dip tomatoes into flour to coat. Then dip tomatoes into milk and egg mixture. Dredge in breadcrumb mixture to completely coat.

In a large skillet, pour 1/2 inch of oil in the pan and heat over a medium heat. Place tomatoes into the frying pan in batches, depending on the size of your skillet. Make sure not to crowd the tomatoes. When the tomatoes are browned, flip and fry them on the other side. Drain them on paper towels.

BLACK BEAN PEACH AND DRUNKEN GOAT CHEESE BITES

Ingredients

- 1 cup black beans, drained and rinsed
- 1 cup diced peeled ripe peaches or canned
- 2 tablespoons minced red onion
- 1 tablespoon minced fresh cilantro
- 1 jalapeño, minced, with or without seeds
- 1 clove garlic, minced
- sea salt, to taste
- black pepper, to taste
- Cajun seasoning, to taste
- 1/4 cup honey goat or drunken cheese
- tortilla chips or phyllo cups

Directions

Combine the beans, peaches, onion, cilantro, jalapeño, and garlic in a medium bowl. Season with salt, pepper, and Cajun seasoning to taste. Serve with tortilla chips or in phyllo cups. Garnish with crumbled goat cheese

SMOKED SALMON MOUSSE CANAPES

Ingredients

- 8 ounces cold-smoked salmon
- 1 (8-ounce) package cream cheese, room temperature
- 2 tablespoons butter, room temperature
- 3 tablespoons half-and-half
- 2 teaspoons fresh lemon juice
- sea salt, to taste
- freshly ground black pepper, to taste
- 1 tablespoon finely chopped fresh tarragon
- pinch of cayenne pepper
- 1 teaspoon Cajun season
- 2 tablespoons dry sherry
- caviar, chopped fresh chives, or parsley as desired for garnish

Directions

Place salmon in a food processor; pulse until finely chopped. Add cream cheese and next 4 ingredients, and process until creamy and fluffy. Add tarragon; pulse until evenly combined. Taste and adjust seasoning, if necessary. (Note: Add more half-and-half if necessary to achieve the desired texture for piping.)

Serve on baguettes, crackers, or English cucumbers or as a dip.

CAJUN CRAB DIP

Ingredients

- 8 ounces crab meat
- 8 ounces cream cheese, softened
- 1/2 cup mayonnaise
- 1/4 teaspoon granulated garlic powder
- 1/4 teaspoon granulated onion powder
- 1/4 teaspoon smoked paprika
- 1/4 teaspoon Cajun seasoning
- sea salt, to taste
- fresh ground black pepper, to taste
- cayenne pepper, pinch
- 1/2 cup sliced green onions
- 1 1/2 cups shredded Monterey Jack cheese
- smoked Gouda cheese

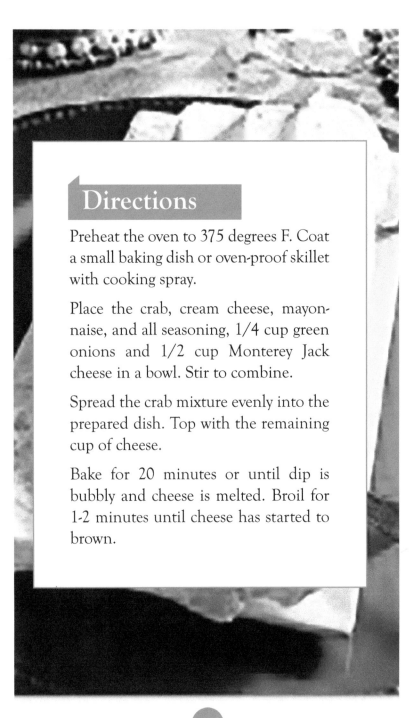

Directions

Preheat the oven to 375 degrees F. Coat a small baking dish or oven-proof skillet with cooking spray.

Place the crab, cream cheese, mayonnaise, and all seasoning, 1/4 cup green onions and 1/2 cup Monterey Jack cheese in a bowl. Stir to combine.

Spread the crab mixture evenly into the prepared dish. Top with the remaining cup of cheese.

Bake for 20 minutes or until dip is bubbly and cheese is melted. Broil for 1-2 minutes until cheese has started to brown.

BRIOCHE FRENCH TOAST

Ingredients

- 1 tablespoon granulated sugar
- 1/2 teaspoon cinnamon
- 1/8 teaspoon fresh nutmeg
- 1 tablespoon flour
- 2 large eggs
- 1-1/2 cup cream or milk
- 1 teaspoon vanilla extract
- 1 teaspoon almond extract
- 1 teaspoon brandy extract

Directions

Whisk together the sugar, cinnamon, nutmeg, and flour.

In a separate bowl, whisk together the eggs, cream or milk, and all extracts.

Whisk the wet ingredients into the dry ingredients.

Soak each piece of bread for about 1 minute on each side, until it has absorbed most of the batter but is not soggy all the way through.

Cook the French toast until it's golden brown. Top with desired fruits and powdered sugar.

CAJUN SPICED BREAKFAST POTATOES

Ingredients

- potatoes, diced
- 1 tablespoon olive oil
- 1 tablespoon butter
- 1 teaspoon sea salt
- 1 teaspoon black pepper
- 1 teaspoon smoked paprika
- 1 teaspoon garlic powder
- 1 teaspoon onion powder
- 1 teaspoon cumin
- 1 teaspoon cayenne pepper
- 1 teaspoon Cajun seasoning
- fresh parsley, chopped

Directions

Preheat cast-iron skillet. Dice potatoes into small cubes. Season potatoes with all the spices. Heat pan and add oil. Add potatoes and spread evenly. Let sit for few minutes to create crust, then turn over and do the same. Continue to turn until desired color and crispness is wanted. Season more if needed. Remove from heat and garnish with fresh parsley.

CAJUN BREAKFAST CASSEROLE

Ingredients

- 6 to 8 eggs
- croissants or brioche bread, diced
- 1 lb ground country and Italian sausage
- onion and bell pepper blend
- smoked Gouda cheese
- salt, pepper, garlic powder, onion powder, paprika, Cajun seasoning

Directions

Layer bottom with bread (to prevent sticking you can spray). Mix eggs and pour over bread and allow to soak. Brown the sausage, onion, and bell pepper until cooked. Add some of the seasoning. Add cheese. Add more sausage mix, seasoning the top with the rest of the cheese. Bake 375 for 20 minutes or until brown.

STRAWBERRY CINNAMON BELGIAN WAFFLES

Ingredients

- 2 1/4 cups all-purpose flour
- 1 tablespoon baking powder
- 3 tablespoons sugar
- 1/2 teaspoon salt
- 1 teaspoon cinnamon
- 1 teaspoon nutmeg
- 2 large eggs, separated
- 1/2 cup vegetable oil
- 2 cups milk
- 1 teaspoon vanilla extract
- 1 teaspoon brandy extract
- 1 teaspoon almond extract
- Strawberry filling:
- 8 to 10 strawberries, hulled and diced
- 1 tablespoon sugar
- 1 teaspoon brandy
- Add strawberries to bowl, add sugar and brandy. Mix well and set aside.

Directions

Preheat your waffle iron and add light oil.

In a bowl, whisk together the flour, baking powder, sugar, salt, fresh nutmeg, and cinnamon.

In another bowl, beat the egg whites with a hand mixer until stiff peaks form. Set aside.

In a separate bowl mix together the egg yolks, vegetable oil, milk, brandy, and almond and vanilla extract.

Add the egg yolk mixture to the dry ingredients and mix well. Next add the strawberries. (Try not to overmix or it will make waffles tough).

Fold in the egg whites gently.

Cook waffles until golden brown. Enjoy!

SMOKED GOUDA FRITTATA

Ingredients

- 1 pint cherry tomatoes
- 1/4 cup heavy cream or milk
- 2 tablespoons olive oil
- 2 tablespoons butter
- 1 bag seasoning blend, frozen
- 2-3 garlic cloves, minced
- 1 teaspoon salt and freshly ground black pepper
- 1 teaspoon cayenne pepper
- 1 teaspoon Creole seasoning
- 1 teaspoon smoked paprika
- 12 ounces mild or hot (or combination of both) Italian sweet sausage
- 8 large eggs
- 1/4 cup grated smoked Gouda
- 1/4 cup grated white Cheddar
- 2 ounces baby spinach

Directions

Preheat the oven to 400 degrees F. Dice tomatoes and set aside. In a bowl mix the eggs, cream, minced garlic, and seasoning; then set aside. Next in a 12-inch skillet (if not nonstick, make sure to grease slightly), cook the sausage until cooked through; then drain on paper towel. Next add olive oil and butter and let melt; then add the frozen seasoning blend and cook until soft. Next add back the sausage and spinach and toss until wilted. Add the tomatoes and gently toss together. Season with little more salt and pepper if needed. Next pour egg mixture into skillet and gently shake to distribute evenly. Sprinkle with the cheese and place in oven. Cook for about 18-20 minutes until set and lightly golden brown.

BUTTERMILK PANCAKES

Ingredients

- 3 cups all-purpose flour
- 3 tablespoons white sugar
- 3 teaspoons baking powder
- 1 1/2 teaspoons baking soda
- 3/4 teaspoon salt
- 3 cups buttermilk
- 1/2 cup milk
- 3 eggs
- 1 teaspoon vanilla extract
- 1 teaspoon almond extract
- 1/3 cup butter, melted

Directions

In a large bowl, combine flour, sugar, baking powder, baking soda, and salt. In a separate bowl, beat together buttermilk, milk, eggs, vanilla and almond extract, and melted butter. Keep the two mixtures separate until you are ready to cook.

Heat a griddle or frying pan with light oil over medium-high heat.

Pour wet mixture into dry mixture, using a wooden spoon or fork to blend. Stir until the two mixtures are just blended together. Do not over-stir! Pour the batter onto the griddle. Brown on both sides and serve hot.

BOURBON SWEET POTATO CASSEROLE

Ingredients

- Casserole:
- 1/2 cup butter (1 stick) at room temperature, plus more to grease pan
- 5 medium sweet potatoes
- 2 large eggs
- 1 cup raw sugar
- 1 teaspoon cinnamon
- 1 teaspoon fresh nutmeg
- 1 teaspoon Jamaican allspice
- 1 1/2 teaspoons vanilla extract
- 1 teaspoon bourbon extract
- 1/2 cup milk
- 1/4 cup bourbon
- pinch of salt
- Topping:
- 1 cup finely chopped pecans
- 1 cup brown sugar, packed
- 1/2 cup all-purpose flour
- 1/4 cup butter (1/2 stick), softened

Directions

For the casserole: Preheat the oven to 350 degrees F. Grease a 2 1/2-quart baking dish with butter.

Poke the sweet potatoes with a fork and bake on a foil-covered baking sheet until they are soft, 1 hour. When cool enough to handle, peel the potatoes, place the flesh in a large mixing bowl and mash until very smooth. Add the eggs, sugar, butter, vanilla and bourbon extract, milk, and salt. Combine well with an electric mixer or hand mixer. Pour the mixture into the baking dish.

For the topping: In a medium bowl, stir together the pecans, brown sugar, flour, and butter until thoroughly combined. Spoon the mixture over the sweet potatoes evenly. Bake the casserole until slightly browned, 40 minutes. Let the casserole sit for 5 minutes before serving.

FOUR-CHEESE MAC 'N' CHEESE

Ingredients

- 6 cups of cooked pasta (I like pasta shells)
- 1 stick of butter
- 4 tablespoons of flour
- 2 cups of half-and-half
- 1 cup of heavy cream
- 1 teaspoon salt
- 1 teaspoon white pepper
- 1/2 teaspoon garlic powder
- 1/2 teaspoon onion powder
- 1/4 teaspoon cayenne pepper
- 4 cups of shredded cheese – your choice: Havarti, Parmesan, white Cheddar, Monterey Jack, smoked Gouda, or sharp Cheddar (or a mix)
- 1/2 cup of sour cream or crème fraîche
- * reserve extra shredded cheese for topping *

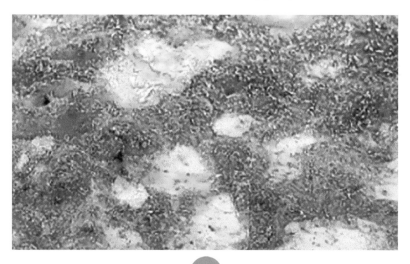

Directions

Preheat the oven to 400 degrees.

For the roux: Melt the butter. Then stir in the flour and cook for about 60 seconds while constantly stirring.

Add in half-and-half and heavy cream and continue to stir periodically while on high heat. When the mixture comes to a boil, it should start to thicken.

Fold in cheese, salt, pepper, garlic powder, onion powder, cayenne pepper, and sour cream/crème fraîche.

Allow the cheese to melt down into a smooth sauce. This should take about 3 minutes on low heat. Mix with the cooked pasta and pour into a baking dish and top with more shredded cheese.

Bake until golden brown.